Voice Training
for the
High School Chorus

Voice Training
for the
High School Chorus

Robert Shewan

Parker Publishing Company, Inc.
West Nyack, New York

© 1973 *by*

PARKER PUBLISHING COMPANY, INC.

West Nyack, N. Y.

Library of Congress Cataloging in Publication Data

Shewan, Robert.
    Voice training for the high school chorus.

    1. Choral singing--Instruction and study.
2. Conducting, Choral. I. Title.
MT930.S52   784.9'62   72-10740
ISBN 0-13-943571-9

Printed in the United States of America

to my wife Nancy

Acknowledgments

An expression of deep gratitude is due to two of my colleagues at Roberts Wesleyan College: first to Judith Coen, instructor in voice and artist-in-residence, for the immeasurable contribution she has made toward the development of the vocal techniques offered in this book; and to William Bippes, professor of art, for his contribution of several illustrations used in the book.

Introduction

Practical Methods for Successful Voice Training

Voice Training for the High School Chorus is principally for high school choral directors. Private and college voice teachers, voice students, and anyone who wishes to expand his knowledge of vocal techniques and their implementation will also find the book helpful. This book is prepared to help you do a more effective job with your chorus. The emphasis is on high school voices, but the approaches are adaptable to all singers of any age. The methods offered have been tried and tested in practice, *and they work*.

In the public schools, frustration is inevitable unless a director makes the best use of time. Time-saving devices that can be used to cope with vocal problems are a major concern of this book. Only techniques that work are presented. All the material in the book has been tested by the author and his students in junior and senior high school choruses, and in college ensembles.

Plain talk comes hard in education, but that's what I want to make. The success of this book depends upon how well you understand it. I hope you sense our talking together – not my simply talking to you. I hope the questions I raise are your questions and the answers eventually your answers. I have sifted the many theories on voice teaching – testing and discarding. What are left are workable guidelines for training choruses to sing better.

High school choral directors should realize that they are primarily voice teachers. College courses in theory, music history and applied music develop musicianship, but the public school teacher cannot transfer his acquired training to his students unless he is able to develop their voices. These are crucial years for students' voices and their musical likes and dislikes.

Performance of great choral literature is largely the responsibility of amateur choruses. Except for performances of a small number of professional groups, much of our choral heritage would be lost if the amateur choir did not exist. One of America's best resources for choral singing is found in the public high school. However, poor voice training and the mediocre music which is often heard in secondary school performances keep this potential from being realized. In fact, more criticism than praise comes upon the high school choral director. Elbert Bellows writes: "More voices are injured during the adolescent period than at any other time. Young people are often asked to sing music that only trained adults should sing. Much of the time, tenors and sopranos are straining and forcing to reach the top tones of a composition – tones they are unable to achieve due to immaturity and lack of training ... Many choral directors constantly strive for brilliant effects through bigness of tone regardless of the cost of the voices".[1] Heavy schedules, lack of sufficient rehearsal time, and the pressure of performances account for much of this type of criticism. Justifiable fault-finding results when a teacher lacks an under-

---

1. Elbert L. Bellows, "Suggestions to the Choral Director," *Music Journal*. Vol. III (March, 1960), p. 54.

standing of the vocal mechanism and is unaware of choral literature suitable for high school voices.

Singing is an involved and complex act involving the whole person. Any person who explains a voice teaching method must, by its nature, break the complex whole into simplistic parts. I do this in the chapters on singing, realizing the necessity to pull all of the parts back together into the holistic method in which I believe.

The chapters on the singing voice include what is mental and what is physical, and what is voluntary and what is involuntary. We waste time when we misinterpret these concepts. Understanding these principles helps simplify teaching procedures and leads to quicker results.

Robert Shewan

Contents

Aural image • Teaching aural image • Developing new speech concepts • Speaking by aural image • How to develop better habitual speaking voices • Developing high speech sounds •

Transferring speech to singing • Mental coordination • Guidelines for imagining a pitch with speech • Four types of singers • Teaching through silent singing • Using the tape recorder • Singing without hesitation or critical judgment • Trusting the imagination to guide the vocal mechanism • Conducting the "Release" beat pattern •

Timbre alternatives in singing • Teaching timbres • Teaching timbre recognition through speech • The descending siren • Teaching chest timbre • Teaching middle timbre • Teaching upper timbres • Singing exercises that help singers find their timbres

How and why aural-image placement works • Singing sensations

• Teaching aural-image placement • The vocal attack • Resonance misconceptions •

CHAPTER 5 – Teaching Expressive Singing, Choral

Teaching students to sing loud *mf-f* • Teaching students to sing soft • Messa Di Voce: the crescendo-diminuendo • Teaching vocal flexibility • Expression in singing • Emotional vitality • Singing with spirit • Teaching intonation • Psychological aspects of intonation • Self-motivation • Spinning tone • Spinning gesture • What does spinning do? • When to use spinning technique • Choral blend •

CHAPTER 6 – Teaching Breathing in the High School

Theories of Vocal Fold Vibration • Breath control misconceptions • Some important scientific findings about breathing • Unnatural breathing • Natural breathing • Directions for correct respiration • Teaching the diaphragm to open and close the thorax • Releasing the breath • How to check your singers' breath release • Conducting the breath • Staggered breathing • Breathiness • Posture • Checking your students' posture • How to maintain good standing posture • How to maintain good seated posture • How to stand from a seated position • Calisthenics •

CHAPTER 7 – Obtaining Good Diction in Voice Training

How to get good diction • Pure vowels and corresponding symbols • Rules for singing vowels • Diphthongs and corresponding symbols • The neutral vowel • The backward diphthong • R's and diphthongs • Consonants • How to teach unvoiced and voiced articulation • Rules for consonants • Emotional diction • Suggestions for an emotional text interpretation • How to get an emotional response from your choristers • Whispering – an auxiliary technique • Latin pronunciation • A Latin pronunciation chart • Release of articulation muscles • Articulation misconceptions • The diagastric muscles •

Voice Training
for the
High School Chorus

CHAPTER 1

Developing Tone Concepts
Through Speech

THE BRAIN CONTROLS all functional motor activities; muscular activity in singing is no exception. Singing originates from a series of speech images and pitch images coordinated in the brain. A singer controls his pitch and speech by sending impulses from the brain to the vocal mechanism, which includes the muscles of the larynx, the respiratory muscles, and the tongue, lip and facial muscles. Singers who sing absolutely silently in their imaginations have motor movement in the lips, tongue and larynx even when they make an effort not to do so.[1] William Vennard has recorded an experiment in which the movement of muscles in the larynx were examined by electromyography. Muscular activity was noted in the laryngeal muscles when the subject was merely thinking pitches. Discussing the cricothyroid muscle, Vennard writes: "Imagine ascending an octave and it [an electromyogram] registers almost as much activity as if you sang it."[2]

---

1. Carl H. Delacato and Anthony R. Flores, "Ideo-Motor Force, An Experimental Rehabilitative Modality," A paper presented before the Rehabilitation Forum (December, 1956).

2. William Vennard, "Letter to the Editor," *The National Association of Teachers of Singing Bulletin*, Vol. XIX, No. 1, (October, 1962), p. 5.

Two nerves connect the brain with the larynx: The right nerve takes a direct path to the larynx while the left nerve loops down around the main artery of the heart (aorta), and then back up to the larynx. The left nerve, because of its proximity to the heart, has been severed during heart surgery. With a severed left nerve the left vocal fold no longer functions. No amount of air passing the vocal fold can cause it to vibrate. The obvious conclusion is that pitch and speech orginate in the neurological processes and not in any direct manipulation of breath and/or body muscles.

Aural Image

All singers sing in their imagination while they sing aloud or they could not sing at all. I refer to singing in the imagination as singing by aural image. Mental messages (aural images), good or bad, are sent to the larynx via nerves—no messages, no sound. The sounds your students imagine in their minds cause neurophysiological adjustments that result in the tones they produce. A deaf person's vocal apparatus is normal, but he cannot produce normal sounds because he has never heard them. He cannot imagine them. How well or how badly one sings depends on four factors: (1) The quality of the singer's speech concepts, (2) the singer's tonal memory, (3) the mental coordination or lack of mental coordination of speech and pitch in the imagination, and (4) how much a singer trusts his ability to sing in the imagination to guide his vocal mechanism.

Teaching Aural Image

Aural image results when we speak or sing silently in the imagination. You can help your choristers learn how to guide their voices by singing in the imagination by teaching them the following steps:

Step 1. *Teach your choristers how they imitate.* Every normal person has some ability to imitate—impersonate. Anyone who can imagine sounds can produce them if they are within his physiological makeup. The most elementary way to teach aural image is by exact imitation—the way an infant learns: he hears, he imagines, he speaks. Have students in your chorus imitate easy animal sounds (dogs, cats, cows, etc.). Ask them how they achieved the imitations. Chances are they will give a physiological answer about some vague idea of the breath causing the vocal cords to vibrate. Ask them what they were *conscious* of doing. The correct answer is: "I merely imagined the sound and then did it." The initial concept is learned. The way we imitate is to imagine sounds silently and then imitate aloud, consciously imagining in our minds the sounds we want to reproduce. Impersonations originate in the imagination.

Step 2. Have your students imitate each other's speech or that of a famous person whose speech has a unique quality (within the appropriate range—boys imitate boys, girls imitate girls). Ask them to concentrate silently on the sound they are going to imitate. Teach them to imagine the sound of another person's voice, then imitate it aloud; if they can't imagine it, they can't imitate it. Imagining speech sounds is the means to the end, the cause of the effect.

Step 3. Have your students 'mock' each other's singing voices or those of well-known singers. Most young people today are great 'mockers.' They listen to a person sing, they imagine the sound, and they imitate—slightly off. Make use of this common trait of adolescents to teach how the vocal mechanism is controlled by the imagination.

Step 4. Explain the neurological processes involved in singing. Tell the students how their vocal mechanisms were innervated by sounds they imagined. In other words, teach your choristers what I wrote in the opening paragraphs of this chapter about mental control of functional motor activity, and teach them to trust this process.

Step 5. Teach your students how to imitate their own speech sounds when they sing. The questions my students often ask me at this point are: "How do we know what we are supposed to sound like? How do we know which tone is really us?" My answer is: imitate your own speech sounds when you sing.   Implement 'self-imitation' by having the choristers speak or shout on a pitch level somewhat higher than their habitual speaking level. Say *ah* or *ee* in a middle pitch area. Have the students imagine the quality and volume of their voices when they speak and then imitate that quality and volume when they sing. Imagine the quality and volume of each speech sound in the imagination on a given pitch and sing. Say *ah* ... imagine a pitch with the speech sound and sing it without critical judgement or hesitation. Do it: don't think about how. The results are twofold: new speech concepts develop as the students speak on pitch levels different from their habitual levels, and the students learn how to imitate their speech sounds when they sing.

First attempts at self-imitation may be difficult and even crude. The important thing to remember is to sing in the imagination the same quality of the speech sound, whether the quality of the speech is good or not. If the speech sounds are nasal and tight, the singing should sound nasal and tight. If the speech is dark, throaty, or bright, the tone should be the same. If the speech is loud, the singing should be loud; if the speech is soft, the singing should be soft. Students experience the how and why of the neurological control of the vocal mechanism through these early attempts to imitate and impersonate. Step one in learning to sing is understanding the role the imagination plays in the singing act. How do we improve the vocal concepts we imagine? We start with the speaking voice. We only need to listen to great singers speak to realize the closeness of speaking to singing. Great singers speak and sing with the same quality—and they speak loudly. They sing well because they speak well — not the other way around.

Developing New Speech Concepts

Free speech results when a student can speak in the imagination the sound he wants to produce aloud. Herein lies the crux of all good speech. (The brain controls all functional motor activities.) In the first stages of our presentation we asked students to imitate by imagination. The more clearly they imagined sounds, the better they could imitate. This concept holds true for speech as well.

Speaking By Aural Image

1. Ask your students to imagine speaking a phrase such as "how are you today" within the pitch area of c^1 inflecting above and below.
2. Do this several times until they can imagine each work loud and clear.
3. Have the choristers speak aloud (without hesitation or critical judgment) letting their neurological processes *cause* the sounds to come out. Be sure they strive to speak each word in the imagination simultaneously with their speaking aloud.
4. Practice on various pitch levels throughout the student's ranges.

How to Develop Better Habitual Speaking Voices

American speech contrasts to speech of other nationalities as flat-sounding and too low in pitch. Laryngologists have a special concern about vocal polyps and other vocal disorders in America resulting from our cultural pattern of uninflected low-pitched speech. Speech scientists teach that every individual has an optimum pitch level for correct speaking. On an individual basis this can be determined by the following empirical method: Have the student speak a short phrase, such as "how are you today," at full volume beginning on middle c (one octave lower for male voices). Inflecting the last syllable (day) downward helps to differentiate speaking on a pitch from singing on a pitch. Be sure the student speaks rather than sings. (See Figure 1-1.)

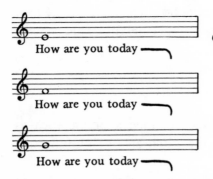

Inflect the final syllable downward as a descending sigh.

Continue speaking on pitches up to c^2 and down below c^1 at full volume until the student recognizes the pitch on which he speaks most easily and you recognize the pitch that sounds most resonant. Continue testing until you and the student agree on the same pitch.

Figure 1-1

The student repeats this phrase full volume up and down the scale until it is determined by you and the student which notes were the easiest to speak on (his diagnosis) and the most resonant sounding (your diagnosis). This area is called the optimum pitch for speaking. Compare these notes with the student's habitual speaking level and then encourage the student to practice reading aloud on the new level inflecting above and below, until it becomes natural to speak there. The axiom—we sing as we speak—holds true for good and bad singing. The quality of singing voices invariably sounds the same as speaking voices. If a student speaks lightly and breathily, he sings that way. If his speaking voice is tight, harsh or throaty, so is his singing voice. Resonant speakers sing with resonance (those who have not learned to compare speech to singing are exceptions).

We all have an optimum pitch level on which we speak with maximum freedom and resonance. Finding this optimum pitch level helps establish resonant speech sounds and vocal freedom. Using it with inflections above and below establishes a mental image of speech sounds that carries over into singing.

Your students can practice speaking on optimum pitch levels in full rehearsals and sectionals, even though subtle individual differences in resonance cannot be heard. Students are less inclined to inhibitions when working in a group, and even in full rehearsals you can find definite pitch areas which are freer and sound more resonant for each section (assuming the voices are correctly classified). Choristers will agree with each other on the pitch area best suited for their section. Trial and error and repetition are necessary until you and your students discern the area we call optimum pitch level.

In Figure 1-2, I have listed the areas in which I generally find optimum pitch levels for each section. I give these only as general rules, since the age and individual maturation of singers slightly varies these findings.

The above pitches represent the average optimum pitch levels within each person.

Figure 1-2

Guidelines:

1. Always speak in a full voice rather than on a conversational

dynamic. Inflect well above and below the optimum pitch level. Speak by aural image.

2. Use a tape recorder so the students can hear the pitch level which *sounds* most resonant to you.

3. Compare the habitual pitch levels with the optimum pitch levels. Note the difference.

4. Encourage students to practice reading on the new pitch level for speaking until it becomes natural.

Once we have established the correct pitch level for full, free speaking, we need to work to establish free speech sounds throughout the vocal range. When we speak much above the optimum speech level we experience a closer affinity to shouting than speaking. Therefore we must teach students how to shout high with free, full sounds.

Developing High Speech Sounds

A high speech sound is projected as in a dramatic production and/or in choral speaking—not the football and basketball yell. All loud high speech sounds must be done by aural image. Loud, high speech often assimilates a free shout or call. Vennard defines *shout* as a "Loud, free cry"[3] and writes: "I find that both men and women benefit from the suggestion 'Sing the way you speak it', or 'Don't sing it so beautifully, shout it'."[4]

Loud, high speech is sighed out rather than pushed out. Teach high speech by shouting a vowel, as a gradually descending siren "ah." Students tend to start shouts with a glottal attack and a tight body. Tell them to *sigh* a loud, descending, full speech sound. Be sure your singers do *not* descend too quickly. A loud sigh teaches correct attacks and helps the students experience muscular release of laryngeal and respiratory muscles.

---

3. William Vennard, *Singing: the Mechanism and the Technic*, Rev. Edition (New York: Carl Fischer, Inc. 1964), p. 122.

When speaking a phrase such as shown in Figure 1-1, the descending siren should be enacted on the final word. Don't expect the students to get it in the first few attempts. All loud sighs should be done by aural image. The final results should be free speech sounds throughout the complete range of the voice, including the highest notes for tenors and sopranos.

Optimum pitch level, loud-sigh and speaking by aural image teach students how to imagine free, full speech sounds throughout their ranges.

We use speech to train the mind to imagine simple vocal sounds. Transferring these speech sounds to singing is the next step.

CHAPTER 2

Guiding Voices by Singing in the Imagination

As we are establishing new speech concepts through aural image, optimum pitch and loud-sigh technique, we should also be teaching our students to imagine singing with the new speech concepts these techniques develop.

Transferring Speech to Singing

The objective here is to show students how to transfer their new speech concepts to singing. Follow these directives:

1. Loud-sigh "ah" within a middle pitch area (approximately C^2 down to G^1). The speech should be free and pure—not chesty or raucous.
2. Sing the pitch B^{b^1} aloud, imitating the sound and volume of the loud-sigh without hesitation or delay between the spoken sound and the sung tone.
3. Do this exercise within various pitch levels and on all the vowels. The students are successful when the sung tone has the same speech timbre, vowel and volume as the speech sound.

There are three steps: A free loud speech sound assimilating the sigh, imagining pitch and speech together in the mind, and the sung tone assimilating the speech sound in timbre, volume and vowel. Our goal is to show the singers how the imagined sounds determine the actual sung tones.

Some students will have immediate success while others will find imitating the speech timbre, vowel and volume in singing difficult. These persons need much repetition and many trial and error attempts before the concept of guiding the vocal mechanism by mental images sinks in.

Mental Coordination

Mental coordination takes place when a singer imagines his pitch and speech images together as one image. Before students can sing consistenly well, they must be able to imagine speech and pitch images as one image without first speaking aloud. Before they can trust the imagination to guide the vocal mechanism, they have to reinforce their ability to imitate speech when they sing. It is a memorization process which results from much repetition.

Vowels

The imagination must contain a clear concept of each vowel sound that the singers intend to sing. As we imagine words silently, the vowels take on distinctive shapes in our imaginations. These shapes become clear in the imagination if we move our mouths as if we were singing aloud. As we concentrate on the imagined sound, the muscles of the mouth are innervated. The muscular action clarifies the shapes of the vowel images in our imaginations. We must not be involved in the mouth movements as such: *these must be a result rather than a cause.* The first attempts might be conscious ones, but the mouth movements will become unconscious as students repeat the process over and over, and as attention is drawn more and more to what's going on in the imagination.

The importance of vowels in guiding the voice by the imagination cannot be overstressed. Vowels are formed by an intricate system of nerves and muscles. Incorrect vowel images cause the wrong muscles to form the vowels. Thus we have singers forming vowels with too much stress on the throat muscles because the lips, tongue and facial muscles are not properly innervated. Overemphasis on relaxation of the lips, tongue and facial muscles causes students to underwork these muscles to the extent that much of the vowel formation usually done by these muscles must be done by the throat muscles.

To avoid this problem I ask students to enunciate when they sing, with the same lip, jaw, tongue and facial movements they use when they speak aloud. For students who need remedial help, I suggest they hold their cheeks and lips forward while they both recite and sing. This merely brings the lip and facial muscles into proper action and eliminates excess throat tension. However, the role of the imagination must not be minimized during the practice.

Guidelines for Imagining a Pitch with Speech

1. Speak aloud on ee ⌒＼or ah ⌒＼.
2. Speak silently the exact timbre, volume and vowel of the speech sound in the imagination.
3. Imitate that speech sound when you sing in the imagination.
4. Sing aloud, without hesitation, letting the imagination guide the sung tone. The imagined sounds are correct when the sung tone exactly imitates the spoken sound and has the same volume as the spoken sound.

At first do not worry about voice quality. If the speech is

ugly, the sung tone should be ugly. If the speech is free and full, the tone will be free and beautiful. The goal here is to teach students to imagine pitch and speech together as one. The better the speech concept, the more beautiful the sung quality will be. Either the tape recorder or another person is needed to record how successfully the students imagined their speech and pitch together (that is, imitated their speech when they sang).

Let me clarify further. There are four types of singers.

Four Types of Singers

The first type, the natural or well-trained singers, sing with full free tones, in tune. These persons have clear, precise images of pitches and vowels; they have good speech sounds and already imagine speech and pitch together in their mind. They sing without inhibitions because they have confidence in their mental processes and let their imagination guide their vocal mechanisms. Some people believe formal training ruins a natural singer's voice. Maybe you have sent a 'natural' to college, only to be disappointed when you heard your prize student several months hence. The beauty of the tone is gone, the smooth vibrato widened and slowed. Even the pitch is not as true. Is the voice ruined? Physically speaking, probably not. What has been ruined is the singer's natural ability to trust his imagination to guide his voice. Emphasis on mechanics and physical technique directed your student's attention away from his natural process of guiding his voice mentally. He has become busy thinking about breathing, how to hold his rib cage, relaxation of his tongue, lips, and jaw, etc. The very thing that made him sing well (aural image) was minimized or lost completely. Once confident and exuberant, he has become self-conscious and introspective about his voice. We all suffer when we experience such a tragedy to one of our own students.

Natural singers need to be taught how they already sing. Teach them first how their imagination controls the vocal mechanism; second, how they can improve their speech concepts; and third, how they can improve their singing by further trusting the mental processes they already use so well. Do not change the naturally correct vowel formations by stressing relaxation of the articulation muscles, or bother the singer with conscious muscular manipulations.

The second type sings full, free, beautiful tones—if and when they learn the pitches. These singers speak without inhibitions, have good vocal timbres, habitually speak in their optimum pitch levels with a wide area of inflections, but have weak pitch concepts. Once they have learned the pitches, they imagine their pitch images with their beautiful speech sounds and the resultant tone is full and free. These singers cause much frustration to directors because they sound so great, if and when they learn the notes. They do not need lessons in voice production but rather need help to develop musicianship.

Sometimes their lack of success stems from an inability to count rhythms. A former student of mine who had a beautiful natural soprano voice had problems learning pitches and difficulty sustaining a pitch without flatting. When she tried to read music she was unable to keep her place. She could not trust her mental images enough to let them do their job. After several months of learning how to count rhythms and how to relate counting to physical movements (eurythmics), her singing improved immensely. She was naturally endowed with good speech sounds and the ability to imagine pitches with them *when* she was rhythmically secure.

Singing silently in the imagination aids singers who have weak pitch images. I have had choristers who were unable to imagine a familiar tune silently for more than two measures before their tonal memory failed. Some years ago during a chorus rehearsal, I heard a rich bass voice booming out from a section that had until that day been relatively weak. After determining who had this "great voice," I asked him to remain after rehearsal. The boy had some music background, played an instrument and was able to count rhythms fairly well. I encouraged him to study voice privately. Only after his first lesson did I discover why I had not noticed him before. Because of a very weak tonal memory it had taken him half of the year to learn the bass notes. What a beautiful speaking voice—and when he knew a song very well he sang beautifully. At first he could not sing a song silently in his imagination for more than two measures. He persevered, practiced singing silently, and stretched his tonal memory until he was able to "sing" for long periods of time in his imagination. Silent practice was not easy: the songs of the first weeks were limited to easy material containing I-IV-V harmonies and simple intervals. The boy worked hard and eventually graduated from college as a voice major and sang very well indeed. Both of these singers were helped by silent practice.

Silent practice helps all singers and should be a part of every chorus rehearsal. Sergius Kagen, a great exponent of aural image, wrote: "Too many voice students waste a great deal of time and energy trying to limber up their voices without first trying to limber up their ability to imagine pitches."[1] Silent practice helped these singers in three ways:

1. It forced them to use their imaginations.
2. It helped them locate their aural images.
3. It exercised the muscles of the singers' vocal mechanisms while they imagined the speech and pitch—especially when they allowed the mouth to move as if they were singing aloud. Again, it is important for this type of student to continue the natural habits of vowel formation and good speech production. Drawing attention to physical aspects of production only complicates the picture and deters the singers from developing those aspects of musicianship they lack—tonal memory and rhythm.

The third type of singer sings in tune but has an unpleasant tone quality—these singers imitate their speech when they sing,

---

1. Sergius Kagen, *On Studying Singing* (New York: Dover Publications, Inc., 1950), pg. 60.

but the speech concepts are of poor quality. Good musicians who play instruments extremely well but have done very little singing often fall into this category. These singers are much easier to help than type two because they already can imagine pitch images and speech images together. They often have inhibitions about using their voices; we have difficulty getting them to speak with any volume. Once they improve their speech quality and vowel concepts, they progress very rapidly. The choral rehearsal gives these individuals a chance to experiment with new speech sounds while they get "lost in the crowd." They rapidly learn to sing better by transferring speech to singing, by guiding the transfer in the imagination.

Type four has poor speech sounds and weak pitch concepts. These students are by far the most difficult to teach. They listen to themselves and try to improve their singing by conscious (physical) means rather than by mental intuition. They need to develop new speech concepts and new pitch concepts as well as learn to trust their imagination to guide their voices. Optimum pitch, loud-sigh and speaking by aural image help them establish free speech concepts. Transferring speech to singing helps develop confidence in the imagination to guide the vocal mechanism.

Briefly: Singer *type one*, the natural singer, already has good speech concepts, he imitates the speech when he sings, and he sings without hesitation or critical judgment, trusting how he "sings" in the imagination to guide his voice.

Type two can be helped only if tonal memory (ability to imagine pitches) is developed through silent singing, and if rhythmic coordination is improved.

Type three is helped when the singers get better speech concepts through speaking by aural image, loud-sigh technique and optimum speech level. Their ability to imitate their speech sounds when they sing is already excellent.

Type four needs all techniques more or less equally—speaking by aural image, optimum pitch level for speaking, loud-sigh for high speech sounds, transferring speech to singing, and silent singing.

Teaching Through Silent Singing

Here is how you can check the clarity of your singers' pitch images. First, have your chorus begin 'singing' a familiar tune silently in the imagination, letting the mouth move as if singing aloud. Signal the chorus to sing aloud after several beats by using some prearranged signal. Check the accuracy of the pitch image by checking the pitch when the chorus sings aloud against the piano or a pitch pipe.

Now check the speech images. Imagined speech contains both timbre and vowel. Have the chorus imagine singing the song silently (letting the mouth move) and ask them if they sang timbre and words as well as pitches. Most of them will imagine vowels and consonants. Do not mistake this for speech timbre. Ask them what the pitches and words *sound like* when they imagine a phrase of a song silently. Many students do not imagine a speech quality when they sing silently. For example, some describe the sounds they imagine as flute-like or even high squeaks. Others say the timbre is too vague to describe. Instrumentalists sometimes imagine the quality of one's instrument which is difficult to reproduce by the voice, to say the least. Most of us imagine the quality of our conversational speaking voice, which may or may not be good.

Tonal memory and speech memory can be developed through silent singing, but this technique is by no means easy for everyone, and sometimes requires time and patience on the part of a teacher and students. The greatest problem facing the fledgling singer who lacks natural mental coordination is learning to concentrate in his imagination. Kagen wrote:

"Learning how to form a series of accurate images of the sounds one wishes to produce may be an extremely tedious and difficult task, one demanding considerable practice and a great degree of self-discipline. It requires at first the utmost of concentration—the kind of concentration which can sometimes be attained only by trying to make one's mind totally blank and substituting a continuous series of sound images for all thought."[2] Singing pitch and speech together in the imagination is difficult for many students. The key lies first in developing clearer pitch and speech concepts, and second, in trusting how we sing in the imagination, through the neurological process, to make the voice come out.

Using The Tape Recorder

Show the students their results by using the tape recorder. Students' feedbacks lie to them concerning what they sound like when they speak and sing. Everyone is surprised when he first hears himself on a recording. Students need to hear what they really sound like compared to what they think they sound like. Often an improved tone quality sounds worse rather than better within the student's own ear. The tape recording tells the truth about progress.

All people have a self-image, and the voice plays a major part in that image. Men darken their tone because a darker tone makes them feel more masculine. Girls sing with a light pinched quality because it makes them feel more feminine. I remember a student, a freshman in college, who had a "little girl" image. As she developed new timbre concepts, her voice quality greatly matured. I asked her how she liked her voice when she heard it on tape. Her reply was, "it shatters me; it isn't me." In a real sense, her self-image had to change before she was psychologically willing to speak and sing with full, free tones. The tape

---

2. *Ibid.* p. 56.

recorder proved the student was a poor judge not only of her own tone quality, but of her true self as well. Below are some examples of students whose feedback lied to them about their true vocal quality. Compare their recorded sound against how they said they sounded to themselves before they heard the recording.

What the Student Thought He Sounded Like (Feedback)	*Tape Playback*
Student heard her voice brighter than it actually was. (Very common)	Dark throaty tone
Student sounded richer to himself than he actually did.	Thin breathy tone
Students' feedback was much darker than the playback. (Very common)	Harsh, strident tone
Students mistook twang for resonance.	Nasal twang caused by tight pharynx
Student heard her voice dark and rich. (Very common)	Bright muscularly pulled up voice

Many more examples could be added to this list. I find I am a better teacher when I know how students think they sound compared to their actual sound. Knowing how they sound to themselves helps me better understand why they sing the way they do, both from the standpoint of vocal factors and in view of psychological factors. The students can get a truer picture of how they sound and how their feedbacks have been fooling them.

The tape recorder is also valuable in helping choristers accept the sound of their voices when they speak on higher, more resonant pitch levels. It is very helpful in teaching them how to transfer new speech sounds to singing. Most students cannot tell if they succeed in imitating the quality and volume of their speech sounds when they sing. Utilize the tape recorder in the following ways: While the tape recorder is on, ask your chorus (or student) to speak, full voice, a phrase of a song on a pitch level which coincides with the tessitura of the phrase. (See Figure 2-1.) The bulk of the notes fall around b. Have your

This Joyful Eastertide

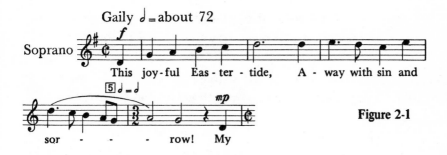

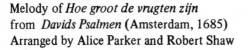

Figure 2-1

Melody of *Hoe groot de vrugten zijn*
from *Davids Psalmen* (Amsterdam, 1685)
Arranged by Alice Parker and Robert Shaw

chorus speak full voice on that pitch. Be sure the singers sigh the syllables, "tide ⌐" and "row ⌐," to establish speech instead of singing. Ask the chorus to then sing the phrase with the same volume and quality as the spoken phrase, guiding their voices by their imaginations. *Speak* the phrase, *sing* the phrase, play the recording back to the students. Repeat this many times until the students can transfer speech to singing by the imagination. Nothing helps students accept an improved tone quality as quickly as practice with the tape recorder, whether in individual or group instruction.

Guidelines:

1. Students should experience transferring speech to singing in their imaginations.

a. Speak aloud *ah* ⌒ or *ee* ⌒ until the speech is free. Preferably choose a speech level in the middle of the voice.
b. Speak in the imagination the same timbre, vowel and volume.
c. Imitate the speech when you sing in your imagination. (Select a pitch that coincides with the pitch level of the speech).
d. Sing aloud without hesitation, letting the singing in the imagination make the resultant sound in the same way we learned to imitate.

2. Check your students' sung tone. If it is exactly the same timbre, vowel and volume of the speech sound the attempt was successful.
3. Speak on different pitch levels and with different vowels until the singer can imitate these speech patterns while singing.
4. Teach the students how they really sound as compared to how they hear themselves through their own feedback.
5. Use the tape recorder to show the students if they are matching the timbre and volume of their speech sounds when they transfer them to singing by imitation.

Singing Without Hesitation or Critical Judgment

Guiding the voices by the imagination is an intuitive act. Teach your students to sing without hestiation and without critical judgment. The following information helps us understand the roles the imagination and intuition have in singing.

The brain has two hemispheres called the dominant and subdominant. Most persons have the dominant sphere on the left side of the brain. The dominant sphere controls our speech mechanisms while singing originates in the right side of the brain (subdominant). It also appears that logical and critical judgment are aspects of the dominant sphere, whereas the subdominant sphere houses our intuitive processes. Much research is still needed to prove conclusively just where in the brain these functions lie or how they work.

We do know that persons who have a stroke in the left side of the brain become paralyzed on the right side of the body and lose some or all ability to speak. In most cases, depending upon the extent of brain damage from the stroke, these persons can still sing. Music, in fact, plays a very important role in the treatment of stroke patients.

The person whose neurological makeup emphasizes musical intelligence is often more intuitive than logical. This trait is important to musicality and to singing particularly. Unfortunately, the educational goals of the past have stressed logic and critical judgment almost exclusive of intuition. Music, a major educational force in developing intuition, is still considered a fringe subject in many schools. Any teaching that stresses physical aspects of singing can lead students away from trusting their intuitive faculties and might even guide students to thinking about singing as a dominant intellectual function. When singing becomes a dominant function, attempts to be expressive end in mechanical interpretation and a tone quality which at its best sounds "arty." *All of the techniques discussed in this book are controlled by singing in the imagination and must be implemented without critical judgment on the part of the singers if they are to experience vocal freedom and if they are to sing expressively.*

All tones must be sung both in the imagination and aloud without any hesitation whatsoever. The instant students imagine a tone, they should sing the tone and sustain it by the imagination. *Imagining the tone and singing are done simultaneously.*

I like to compare singing without hesitation to the toss of a frisbee or flat disc, a game very popular with young people. To get a good frisbee toss, the thrower watches the person he wants to throw it to and lets go instantly. An instant release without physical tension in the arm or wrist causes the disc to float and spin through the air. Singers who sing in the imagination and aloud simultaneously, and sustain the singing in the imagination until the instant of the next note, sing tones that float and spin.

If we throw a frisbee with too much physical effort, it wobbles and drops quickly to the ground. Similarly, a pushed voice often wobbles (or lacks all vibrato) and has little carrying power. We can't forcibly toss a frisbee and get a good throw, nor can we force the voice and get a free tone. We should imagine the sung tone and sing simultaneously by intuition.

As students develop their ability to sing in the imagination, they learn to trust the imagination to guide their voices when they sing aloud. Telling the students to sing without hesitation helps them to trust their mental processes, leaving no time to judge. Sing in the imagination and aloud simultaneously without hesitation. This is one of the keys to teaching students to trust their neurological processes to guide the vocal mechanism.

Trusting the Imagination to Guide the Vocal Mechanism

What does trusting the imagination to guide the vocal mechanism mean? First, it means that we trust the muscular activity of singing to result from the sounds we imagine. Second, it means we imitate our speech sounds when we sing without critical judgment of the process of singing or the sound of the sung tones themselves while we are singing. Third, *we are never anxious about what we have just sung, or what we are about to sing.*

Guiding the voice by singing in the imagination means we imagine the sound we want to produce *when* (the instant) we sing that sound—not an instant before—but simultaneously with the sung tone. We then sustain the tone by continuing to sing in the imagination, and imagine the next tone *when* (the instant) we sing the next tone. We know the next tone is in our tonal memory. We don't have to anticipate it.

Conducting the "Release" Beat Pattern

This beat pattern is done with a relaxed toss of the hand on each beat—like tossing a small ball in each direction of the beat. In Figure 2-2 are two patterns: The toss beat pattern is part A, and the traditional bounce beat pattern is part B. (See Figure 2-2.)

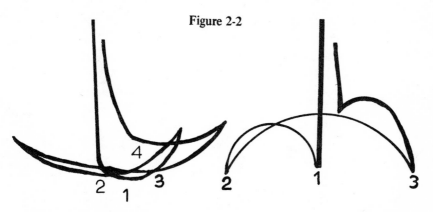

Figure 2-2

Figure 2-2a represents the toss beat pattern; Figure 2-2b represents the bounce beat pattern.

The toss beat helps break a singer's habit of swelling each note. The toss beat also forces the choir to sing the instant it imagines the tone; as a result, each singer implements his aural image technique without hesitation.

Any chorus that contains voices that wobble benefits from imagining the tone being tossed lightly without hesitation. Singing the tone with a light toss eliminates the wide vibratos that are often prevalent in church choirs. The direction to lightly toss the sung tone in the imagination forces singers to trust their imaginations and helps singers overcome physical tensions when they begin a tone; this thought pattern doesn't leave time to tense muscles or to bring critical judgment into play.

Singers who labor each note are involved in listening to themselves (critical judgment). This type of singer generally swells on each note, and consequently lacks musical line. The singer who sings in the imagination and aloud simultaneously, and keeps singing in the imagination without critical judgment, not only has freedom of attack and vocal flexibility, but he sings in a manner which keeps his audience attentive. Keep listening. Something exciting is going to happen.

CHAPTER 3

Establishing Registers—

The Timbres of the Voices

EVERY NORMAL PERSON can speak and sing with three or more different timbres. These different timbres are often referred to as registers. The term "register" was borrowed from the pipe organ nomenclature of the early seventeenth century to distinguish the different timbres of the singing voice. Most voice scientists today believe voices have three or more registers, which they call chest, middle, and head and/or falsetto. Some voice authorities claim there is a *passagio* (passageway) connecting two registers, the chest and head. This *passagio* usually encompasses the same notes which others call middle register. No matter what we call them, the fact remains that every normal person has the potential to speak and sing with several different timbres which are inherent in their voices and which relate to pitch and volume.

Timbre Alternatives in Singing

1. The poorest alternative is the heavy, harsh singing which results from imitating lower speech timbres on high pitches.

Aesthetically this is not only the least satisfying, but continual singing in this way is injurious to the vocal mechanism. When a chorus director allows his singers to carry lower timbres up too high, he can expect a constant problem of flatting and will be disappointed by a lack of dynamic variation. The dynamic range is limited to *mf-f.*

2. A second alternative results from imagining pitches with the upper speech timbres throughout the ranges of the voices. The tone quality of these choirs is often pleasing enough, but they lack a wide dynamic range and have little variation of tone color. There is more danger of sharping than flatting, and tones are usually straight-sounding or contain hints of tremolo. A blend can be easily obtained through this vocal approach, and nondramatic *a cappella* repertoire can be aesthetically satisfying. Danger of injuring the vocal mechanism is less, but the singers are not developing the speech concepts necessary for vocal fulfillment.

3. The third alternative is the correct one. Choristers sing in the imagination appropriate pitches with the designated timbres. These choruses have a full dynamic range and have the ability to color the tone quality when musical expression demands it. They are not as limited in the repertoire they can do, for they have both lyric and dramatic capabilities because they recognize and use the different speech timbres inherent in their voices. Oren Brown writes: "If a voice sounds in the middle of its range the same way that it does in its lower tones, we are sure to have found a cause for strain. So also in the top voice as compared with the middle. Strain is evidenced when any lower qualities are carried too high."[1] Brown says strain results from carrying low timbres up; that is, chest timbre into the middle pitch level or middle timbre into the upper pitch levels. Carrying pure upper speech timbres downward below the designated pitch lev-

---

1. Oren Brown, "Causes of Voice Strain in Singing", *National Association of Teachers of Singing Bulletin*, Vol. XIV, No. 4, (1958) p. 21.

els results in soft singing. There is not the strain in carrying the timbre down as there is in carrying the timbre up, and the tone is more pure sounding. Because of these factors, many high school choral conductors vocalize downward from the upper timbres and acquire a tone that sounds comparatively free, even though the quality lacks fullness and natural resonance. When choruses, which sing by carrying upper timbres downward, attempt a forte, the voices are usually pushed to the point of straining. The only answer for them is to always sing softly—not a very good aesthetic answer.

Teaching Timbres

I prefer to call the registers of the voice chest timbre, middle timbre and upper timbres. When we sing full voice (mf-f) throughout or range, we imitate chest speech timbre on low pitches, middle speech timber on medium pitches, and upper timbres on high pitches. (See Figure 3-1a.) Figure 3-1a shows

Figure 3-1a

Soprano and tenor (8va.) ranges and corresponding timbres.

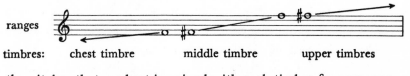

the pitches that are best imagined with each timbre for sopranos and tenors (an octave lower). These timbres vary in range depending upon voice classification. (See Figure 3-1b.)

Figure 3-1b

Mezzo-soprano and baritone (8va.) lower.

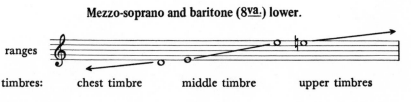

Figure 3-1c

Contralto and bass (8$\underline{\text{va}}$.) lower.

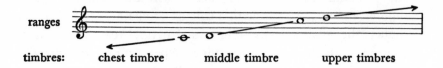

ranges

timbres: chest timbre   middle timbre   upper timbres

Figures 3-1a and 3-1b also include the pitches most authorities agree are the transition notes on which singers change timbres when they are singing full volume.

Teaching Timbre Recognition Through Speech

Chest timbre results when we speak loudly and raspily on a low pitch level; speaking full, clear tones on middle pitches distinguishes the middle timbre from the chest; high, shrill speech helps establish high timbre concepts, $\underline{f}\#^2$ -C^3 .

The Descending Siren

A way to teach your chorus that there are different speech timbres is to shout *nee* or *nah* on a downard siren, starting on $\underline{a}^2$ and descending the whole width of the range while maintaining a forete dynamic throughout the siren. You will hear the timbres change as the singers go below each transition note. Have half the chorus do the downward siren while the other half listens. Use outstanding individual students to demonstrate for others.

Teaching Chest Timbre

Girls who are uninhibited about speaking loudly usually speak in chest timbre, the easiest timbre to discern and teach. Ask your female students to yell as they do at football and basketball games. Yelling this way reveals their chest timbre. The sound is raucous and raspy. Boys, too, can speak in chest timbre, but the quality is more distinctive in the female voices. The use of this quality should be limited to the pitch area below $\underline{f}^1$ for sopranos and $\underline{f}$ for tenors, and $\underline{e}^{b\,1}$ and $\underline{d}^1$ for the lower voices (8$\underline{va}$ for baritones and basses).

Teaching Middle Timbre

Middle timbre is obvious when compared to chest timbre. Ask your students to inflect speech around pitch $\underline{c}^2$ on the phrase, "how are you today," or some similar phrase. Note the difference in sound from chest timbre. Listen carefully to discern that there is *no* chest timbre in the speech sound. A pure middle speech sound is clear sounding and full. If the speech is harsh and raucous, the middle timbre is mixed with chest timbre. If the speech is breathy, the middle timbre is mixed with upper timbre. There is never any breathy quality in pure timbres. If the speech is light and clear, the students are speaking in upper timbers. Always guide speech by speaking by aural image. Speak silently, letting the mouth muscles move, then speak aloud. Students with natural endowment invariably relate the correct timbre to each pitch area when they speak silently. Others can learn by imitation and trial and error. Your example and/or the example of other students is important to timbre discernment.

Briefly, speaking in chest timbre resembles loud speaking in a low pitch area and sounds raucous and ugly. Speaking in middle timbre is clear and bell-like. Performers from England habitually speak in middle timbre.

Teaching Upper Timbres

The upper timbres resemble pure, high, shrill-like sounds. Sometimes imitating a high-pitched siren helps direct the singers to the sound of their upper timbres. Speaking high is more difficult than shouting high at first. Have the students sigh aloud nee⟍ or nah⟍ on a high $\underline{g}^2$ or $\underline{a}^2$. Because of the narrow range of the upper timbre, $\underline{f\#}^2$ including $\underline{b}^{b2}$, the sigh cannot encompass many notes.

You can also establish the timbres of the voice by having your students repeat any spoken phrase up and down the scale until you have included the whole range of spoken possibilities. This technique is similar to establishing optimum pitch areas, except now we intentionally include the extremes of the vocal range. Have the sopranos and tenors start speaking on $\underline{c}^2$ and repeat the phrase with inflection until the whole range has been encompassed. Maintain a full dynamic level—not shouting, but speaking as in dramatic speech. Listen carefully as the students speak through the transition notes. The students, in order to maintain an equalization of volume, will change to chest voice on $\underline{f}^1$ when they descent and on $\underline{f\#}^2$ as they ascend. Point out these changes of quality to the students. Have some speak as others listen. Start the altos and basses a minor third lower. The transition from one timbre to another should approximate those given in Figure 3-1b. The key is maintaining the volume as the students ascend and descend. Any sudden increases or decreases in volume invalidate the technique. *Give each repeat of the phrase by singing in the imagination.*

Speak in the imagination at the desired dynamic level. Speak aloud, letting the imagination guide the speech. Repeat until the quality distinctions of each timbre become clear.

Discerning the various timbres of the voice is crucial for a wide range, for vocal freedom, and for dynamic flexibility. Have your chorus read silently and aloud the texts of the compositions they are going to rehearse at various pitch levels within the appropriate timbres. *This practice should become an important part of each rehearsal.*

As soon as some of the students can speak the words of a composition with the correct timbre, have them sing on the written pitches, imitating the speech sound as they sing. Remind them to guide their voices by their imaginations. Speak aloud, and transfer the new speech concepts to singing in the imagination and aloud simultaneously. Be free to fail. Speak the phrase and try again.

A timbre is pure when the brightness of the tone is on the top. When brightness is on the bottom of the tone, the timbres are mixed (the lower timbres carried up and mixed with upper timbres). When a tone lacks brightness, the timbres are mixed (the upper timbres brought down and mixed with the lower timbres). Pure timbres insure freedom within the vocal mechanism.

Listen to the placement of the vocal brightness in the voices while your students speak aloud and use the loud-sigh technique. Demonstrate the three possibilities spoken and sung: brightness in the bottom of the tone, brightness removed from the tone, and brightness in the top of the tone (the correct tone).

It is just as important to read and sing silently in the imagination as it is to read and sing aloud. For example, in a section with high notes ($\underline{f}\#^2$, $\underline{g}^2$, $\underline{a}^2$), ask the sopranos to (1) imagine themselves speaking the phrase silently with the quality of the upper timbres; (2) imagine themselves singing the phrase silently with the given pitches; (3) after doing this several times have the students sing aloud, guiding their voices by singing in their imaginations. The silent singing in the imagination gives singers the confidence they need to trust the imagination when they sing aloud.

Singing Exercises That Help Singers Find Their Timbres

Modified Vowels: A technique which helps both male and female singers find the correct timbre for the high pitches of their voices is as follows: vocalize upward on *ah* from a pure middle timbre to the transition notes ($\underline{f}\#$ for sopranos and tenors 8va., <u>d</u> for mezzo-sopranos and baritones, <u>c</u> for contral-tos and basses), and change the vowel to *aw* on the transition note. Many of the singers will automatically change into the upper timbre. The same exercise can be done with *ee*, changing to *ih* on the transition pitches. (See Figure 3-2.)

Figure 3-2

ah - - - - - aw - ah - - - - - - - - ah - - - aw - - - ah - - -
ee - - - - ih - ee - - - - - - - - ee - - - - ih - - ee - - -
ay - - - - eh - ay - - - - - - - ay - - - - eh - - ay - - - -

Change to a closed vowel on the upper pitches. This often causes an automatic change from middle to upper timbre. The middle timbre must remain pure until the transition note for the exercise to work.

Falsetto: Have your male students sing falsetto on a given high pitch (<u>d</u>^{1} and above for baritones and bases, <u>f</u>#^{1} and above for tenors) and crescendo until the tone changes into the mature male quality. Some boys will break into the middle timbre, but those who can go through a smooth transition will find themselves singing a beautiful free upper timbre. The pitch must be coordinated to the timbre as the change is made. No more energy should be utilized in the mature tone than was used in the falsetto. Crescendo the falsetto as much as possible before changing to the upper timbre. (See Figure 3-3.)

Figure 3-3

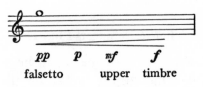

    pp   *p*   *mf*   *f*
   falsetto   upper timbre

Crescendo the falsetto as much as possible, then change to upper timbre. This is an excellent exercise for your tenor section. When the change from falsetto to upper timbre is smooth the exercise is correct. If a break occurs when the change is made the transition is to middle timbre. When this happens the exercise is invalid.

Using the Hum to Teach Timbres: Some singers benefit from humming with the three main timbres on one pitch. The chest voice hum is the buzziest-sounding and loudest, the middle hum is buzzy but lighter than the chest hum, and the upper timbre is lightest with very little buzzy quality. Those who can distinguish the different timbres in their humming can open the three different hums into speech—maintaining the timbre of the hum. Choose a pitch around g^1 or a^1 because they can be hummed in chest voice (loud and raucous), middle timbre (clear and full), and upper timbre (sweet, light and pure).

In order to distinguish timbres you must constantly compare one against the other.

Summary: There are many ways to teach vocal registration. Most teachers do it either by imitation, vowel modification, breath lifts at transition points, or by psychological means (teaching that there are no register changes in the voice). I have found that speech discernment is a natural approach to the establishment of the different timbres throughout the singers' vocal ranges. As the students read up and down the scale within different pitch levels, the imagination automatically tells them to change quality when they reach certain pitches. I have not found this to be as true with singing as with speaking. Again, the mind controls the vocal action and training is done at this level with a minimum of physical directions.

Guidelines

1. As soon as students understand how the vocal mechanism is

guided by mental images (Chapter One) and have learned to transfer speech to singing in the imagination (Chapter Two), the different timbres of the voice should be taught.

2. The descending siren exercise helps clarify the timbre changes in voices, and where the timbre changes take place.

3. Each timbre area has a distinctive quality. Speaking loud, clear sounds in the different pitch areas of the voice helps students recognize the quality that is unique to each timbre.

4. Setting models is very helpful. Have the girls imitate a girl student who speaks easily throughout her range, and the boys imitate a boy student who has clear speech sounds throughout his range. Tenors imitate tenors, baritones imitate baritones, etc.

5. Registers, like all concepts in this book, must be kept in perspective of the final goal of guiding the voice by singing in the imagination. Any technique that detracts from this goal is harmful. We try to help students discover the aural concepts they have to begin with. From these concepts we build, refine, and more clearly define the sounds they imagine.

6. We can sing aloud only what we can sing in the imagination. We fail to sing aloud what we sing in the imagination when we don't trust our imaginations to guide our voices. Instead of trusting, we think about what's coming next or what we have just sung rather than the precise rhythmic pulse we are singing. We must learn to imagine and sing instantaneously and simultaneously, and sustain each tone until the instant of the next pitch—in exact rhythm.

7. Eventually your singers will be able to discern timbre changes while they speak and sing silently. When they reach this level of discernment they no longer need to modify the vowels at the transition points. Instead of the modified vowel causing the timbre change (see Figure 3-2), the timbre change will result from a clear recognition of the timbres while singing in the imagination.

8. The concept of timbre changes needs to be taught and must become a recognizable factor in the singer's imagination before he can gain complete confidence in guiding his voice by imagined sound, the neurological approach to singing.

Chapter Four discusses still another way that can lead singers to a clearer concept of the role singing in the imagination has in guiding the vocal mechanism.

CHAPTER 4

Teaching Aural-Image Placement and Resonance

"Place the voice," "focus the tone," "sing in the masque"—what does it all mean?

Scientists say there is no such thing as voice placement. The larynx cannot be transplanted, nor can the air column be directed into the head, chest or masque; vibrations originate in the larynx and resonate in the laryngeal and oral pharynxes and in the mouth. As Douglas Stanley puts it: "Voice is in the throat—it cannot be 'placed' or 'put' anywhere."[1] Yet for centuries successful singers and teachers have taught voice placement. What do they mean when they say, place the voice?

While a physical placement of the voice is obviously impossible, singers can and do imagine pitches and speech timbres in different parts of the neck, mouth and head. The results are exactly what "voice placers" want. For example, imagining the tone singing in the masque neurologically adjusts certain muscles of the larynx so that a bright forward sound results. Imagining the voice singing at the nape of the neck neurologically adjusts other laryngeal muscles and a dark, "open throat" sound results. Teachers who say "focus the voice

---

1. Douglas Stanley, *Your Voice, Applied Science of Vocal Art* (New York: Pitman Publishing Corp., 1945), p.4.

forward" should say, "sing more forward in the imagination;" teachers who say, "place the voice deep in the chest" should say, "imagine your voice *singing* in the chest."

How And Why Aural-Image Placement Works

Figure 4-1 shows some of the placements voice teachers use and recommend.

Figure 4-1

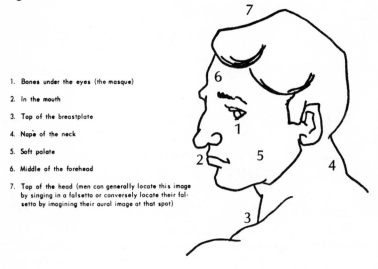

1. Bones under the eyes (the masque)

2. In the mouth

3. Top of the breastplate

4. Nape of the neck

5. Soft palate

6. Middle of the forehead

7. Top of the head (men can generally locate this image by singing in a falsetto or conversely locate their falsetto by imagining their aural image at that spot)

Drawing of a head with seven numbered sections.

Each time we sing in our imagination at a different placement, physiological changes take place within the vocal mechanism which in turn determine the tone color of our voice. The effects of singing in the imagination at these placements are: Number 1 produces a tone that is bright and forward-sounding, and is best for high notes (upper timbres); number 2 sounds round and open and is best for medium pitches (middle timbre); number 3 has a hard metallic quality much like that of many Italian singers and is best for low pitches (chest timbre); number 4 has a darker quality, and is conducive to middle timbres in lower voices; number 5 tends to be dark and muffled; it is used as a pseudo-covered tone by some choral directors (sing in the yawn, or sing through an *aw*); number 6 causes a sound usually referred to as head tone and used for *mezza voce;* number 7 produces a light head tone (very "falsettoish" in men's voices).

Singing Sensations

Many good singers claim they guide their voices by anticipating sensations in a specific placement. What these singers actually do is unconsciously imagine themselves singing in the placement where they feel the sensations. The sensations they feel are a result, not a cause. Aural-image placement caused the sensations. Striving for sensations puts the cart before the horse; therefore, vocal problems result. Here's why:

1. Physical tension often results when beginning singers strive for sensations. For many, "place the voice here" or "focus the voice there" psychologically implies a physical action.
2. A novice has never experienced the "correct" sensations, so he has no idea what to anticipate. He tries physically to obtain the intangible sensations.
3. Voice teachers differ as to what singing sensations feel like.
4. When a singer has a cold or other physical ailments, his sensations vary.

Singers and teachers who use the placement-sensation approach are mistaken in their analysis of what is actually happening. They speak in terms of anticipating sensations at a given place in the anatomy; they should speak in terms of singing in the imagination at the desired placement and let the sensations happen.

Aural-image placement is a cause; sensations are a result. Saying "place the tone (voice) in the masque" *might* lead some singers to imagine singing there. When such accidental aural-image placement happens the teacher's goal is satisfied, but this is like going around the barn to get in the door. Better to say, "*imagine* your pitches and speech singing in the masque." This is direct; the teacher is now working with the cause, not the result.

Briefly, voice placement is unscientific and, except in cases where students, by accident, mentally switch their aural images to the desired placement in the imagination, results in physical tension. When imagined speech and pitch images innervate the muscles of the vocal mechanism, no physical tension is necessary.

Teaching Aural-Image Placement

We have already discussed how we imitate speech sounds when we sing. We have learned that freedom of vocal production depends on the extent to when we *trust* imagined sounds to guide the vocal mechanism. Make no attempt at teaching your students to imagine speaking and singing in different placements until they fully understand and implement the material in the foregoing chapters. Let us reveiw the teaching steps which lead to aural-image placement:

1. Teach neurological control of the vocal mechanism through imitation and impersonations. (Chapter One.)
2. Teach free speech sounds through optimum pitch level, by speaking by aural image and loud-sigh technique. (Chapter One.)
3. Teach transferring speech to singing by imitating speech while singing. (Chapter Two.)
4. Teach the different timbres of the range and imagine appropriate pitches with each speech timbre. (Chapter Three.)

5. Introduce aural-image placement; that is speaking and singing in the imagination at specific anatomical placements. (Chapter Four.)

I have learned empirically that when I sing in the imagination at different placements in the anatomy (in the mouth, in the head, in the masque, etc.), the vocal color of my voice changes. Empirically, singers through the centuries have discovered that "thinking" their voices in the masque resulted in a bright, ringing tone, "thinking" their voices in the back of the neck resulted in a dark, somber tone, etc. You can help your choristers experience these phenomena. Select a phrase of a song your choristers already know which has a tessitura around $\underline{a}^1$. Now direct them as follows:

1. Press your fingers on the bones under your eyes (aural-image placement).

2. Speak aloud by imagining your voice behind the area where your fingers are pressing.

3. Speak silently in the imagination where your fingers are pressing.

4. Sing silently at the desired placement, imitating the speech sounds.

5. Sing aloud letting your singing in the imagination guide your voice to where your fingers are pressing. Sing without hesitation or critical judgment. The singing action and the imagined sound must be simultaneous. Go through the same process, speaking and singing the phrase at other aural-image placements. Imagine each word and pitch the instant you sing and let the tone result. When the students are successful we hear both different tone colors and different levels of intensity. The results depend on the aural-image placement and the pitches they are singing. It must be done intuitively, not intellectually.

The Vocal Attack

Aural-image placements are the areas in the anatomy where

singers should imagine *their tones begin*. Never think of bringing the voices to the image placement. Physical tension results when one thinks of bringing the tone forward to the mouth or to the masque. Freedom results when singers imagine the tones singing in the mouth or in the masque. This again points up a difference between aural-image placement and the traditional concept of voice placement by sensation.

Guidelines:

1. The place in our anatomy where we imagine our voice speaking and/or singing determines the tilt of the larynx and the muscular adjustments, which in turn determine the timbre with which we sing on any given pitch.

2. Each vowel image has a slightly different location within each aural-image placement. Do not try to imagine every vowel image into the same location. Sing silently and let the imagination determine the vowel placement. Never force a placement. Our goal is to help each student find his true aural-image, not impose one on him.

3. Silent singing, moving the mouth muscles as if singing aloud, is the best way to establish where in the anatomy we imagine our aural images.

4. The singing voice should move up and down between the chest and the masque in the imagination. It is helpful to admonish your students to think up as they sing down and vice versa. A constant reminder to think in the opposite direction of thy ptich movement helps to keep the middle and lower aural images in the mouth area and the higher images in the area behind the cheek bones. Otherwise students imagine their images down too low when the singers descend and too high when the singers ascend.

5. "Pretending" that they sing in a particular placement often directs singers' voices to the correct aural-image placements. We mentally pretend they are there. Pretending is another way to

help students guide their voices by their imaginations (neurologically).

6. The singer should be taught that all muscular activity in the larynx is a result. The muscles of the vocal mechanism are controlled neurologically, not by any conscious muscular control. The muscles of the larynx go into action as a result of the sounds we imagine.

7. All the foregoing concepts must be implemented as one coordinated action. We sing in the imagination in the desired placement and aloud at the same instant. The image placement, the mouth movements, and the singing attack are one action.

8. Finally, all acts of singing by the imagination must be implemented by the singer's will. The imagined sound guides the vocal mechanism, but the singer wills the imagined sounds into the anatomical placements he desires. The singer's will tells the imagination what to do. Otherwise he is controlled by all the speech and pitch habits developed over his lifetime and imbedded unconsciously in his imagination. Guiding the voice by singing in the imagination is a matter of mind over body.

Resonance Misconceptions

Sometimes our students mistrust the aural-image technique because of misconceptions about resonance factors in the voice. Pushing, pulling and straining often result from students' misunderstandings about resonance. The following list includes some common misconceptions:

1. *Misconception*: a tone with the greatest number of overtones (partials) is the most resonant tone.

Fact: Too many overtones create a dissonance with the fundamental; singers sound harsh and strident. Unpleasant-sounding singers need to limit the overtones that emanate from the larynx and resonate in the resonance cavities. Soft, weak, and breathy singers, on the other hand, need to develop speech sounds whereby they can sing with more overtones.

2. *Misconception*: resonant singing requires more physical effort than resonant speaking.

Fact: A good speaking voice has approximately the same number of partials as an equivalent singing voice.

3. *Misconception*: the more sensations a singer feels in his head, the more resonant his tone.

Fact: Sympathetic vibrations of hard surfaces have little effect on resonance. Head sensations are at best an indicator to the singer that he does not have too many overtones on his voice. Too many overtones in his voice negate sympathetic vibrations (the overtones cancel each other out). Ruth writes: "Sounding waves with less overtones have a stronger influence on the hard palate, thereby creating a more beautiful sounding tone."[2] Sensations indicate that a good balance between overtones and fundamental sensations are a result, not a cause.

4. *Misconception*: Hard surfaces are the primary influence on resonance.

Fact: Cavities with soft surfaces have greater influence on resonance. The main sources of resonance are in the larynx cavity itself, the laryngo-pharynx, the oro-pharynx, and the mouth cavity. (See Figure 4-2.)

Hard surfaces are static. We have no influence over them. A hard surface vibrates sympathetically *only* when an overtone is exactly in tune with it. The soft walls of the laryngo-pharynx and oro-pharynx permit a wide range of fundamentals to pass through undampened and add their own frequencies as overtones. There is no need to push the voice forward or strive for "forward resonance."

5. *Misconception*: Nasal and sinus cavities are important resonators.

Fact: The vibrating air column emanating from the larynx is directed into the mouth by the closing action of the soft palate raised against the oro-pharynx (as shown in Figure 4-2).

---

2. Wilhelm Ruth, "The Cause of Individual Differences in Sensation of Head Resonance in Singing," *National Association of Teachers of Singing Bulletin*, (OCtober, 1966), p. 21.

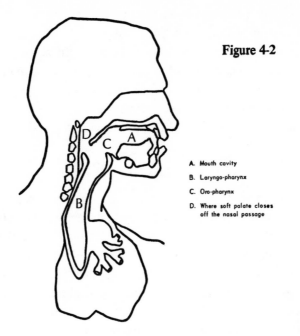

Figure 4-2

A. Mouth cavity

B. Laryngo-pharynx

C. Oro-pharynx

D. Where soft palate closes off the nasal passage

Bisectional drawing of a head with four lettered sections.

Vennard relates an interesting experiment in which five singers performed first normally, and then with their nasal cavities filled with gauze and their sinus cavities more than half filled with water. The difference between the former and the latter performances were negligible to the voice experts who listened. When sentences with nasal consonants were attempted, the differences were obvious.[3] A tone directed into the nasal passage sounded muffled and honky. A similar vibrating air column which moves naturally into the mouth by the neurological closure of the soft palate sound clear and bell-like.

Knowledge of guiding the voice by singing in the imagination eliminates students' attempts to force resonance into voices by

---

3. William Vennard, "Letter to the Editor" *National Association of Teachers of Singing Bulletin,* (October, 1962), p. 6.

physically placing voices forward to obtain resonance. A free, full speech sound is a resonant sound. Resonance in singing results when free speech is transferred to singing. This mental act simultaneously sets the muscles of the vocal mechanism into action. The more we guide physical actions in singing by singing in the imagination, the better chance we have to realize the resonance that is natural to our individual physical makeup.

SUMMARY

Good speech (and singing) results when students imagine their speech sounds inside the anatomical structures of the chest, throat, mouth, masque and head. Generally speaking your students will imagine chest voice inside the chest, middle timbre inside the mouth, and upper timbres behind the masque and behind the forehead. But the higher voices will imagine speech timbres higher in these areas than the lower voices. Our job is to help students discover their natural aural-image placements through speech. Tell your singers to imagine their speech sounds inside of themselves and the words as large as possible. Then ask them to tell you where inside the anatomy they imagined their speech. This is the best way to determine where their *natural* aural-image placements are.

CHAPTER 5

Teaching Expressive Singing,
Choral Intonation and Blend

HOW DO WE unite the technical aspect of singing by the imagination into a singing act which expresses an artistic whole? Expressive singing is more than free, beautiful tone. It requires a wide dynamic range, flexibility of movement and expression—that quality I refer to as the inner spirit of singing.

Teaching Students to Sing Loud _mf-f_

In Chapters Two and Three we learned how to imitate full speech sounds when singing and the importance of transition notes to maintain volume. Review these guidelines to obtain loud, free singing:

1. Teach your students to imitate the speech timbre changes on the transition notes as they sing ascending and descending scales.
2. Teach your students to switch aural-image placements in their imaginations on the transition notes as they sing an ascending and descending scale.
3. Teach students to speak full voice in each of their speech timbres until they experience freedom throughout their ranges.

Speak even the highest pitches (b^2 and above for sopranos, octave lower for tenors). Most authorities consider this area a fourth register; I will refer to it as the *upper upper timbres.*

What happens when singers do not change timbres on the transition notes?

1. Singers who carry lower timbres upward beyond the transition notes sound harsh and heavy.
2. Singers who imagine the timbre change several pitches below a transition note sound like they have "holes" in their voices—that is, areas that are very weak as compared to the rest of their vocal range.
3. Singers who sing a descending scale, starting forte on top and changing timbres several pitches below a transition note, experience sudden decreases and increases in dynamics.

An even scale sung forte throughout requires that singers *imagine* timbre changes on the transition notes suitable for their voice classification. Sing the changes in the imagination; don't make them.

Teaching Students To Sing Soft

Soft singing results from (1) imitating middle speech timbre on low pitches, (2) imitating upper speech timbre on medium pitches, and (3) imitating upper upper speech timbre on high pitches.

Figure 5-1

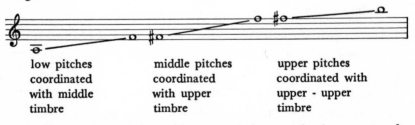

low pitches	middle pitches	upper pitches
coordinated	coordinated	coordinated with
with middle	with upper	upper - upper
timbre	timbre	timbre

Coordinating low pitches with upper timbres results in correct soft singing technique.

Singing upper timbres downward below transition notes causes a decrease in volume. Pure soft singing results.

1. *Singing middle timbres downward into the low pitch area ($f\#^1$ and below)*: Have your chorus *speak* an *ah* or *ee* siren beginning around a^1 (octave lower for boys) and descending to a. Get softer as the siren descends. The timbre of the voices does not change if the volume is sufficiently descreased as the chorus descends below $f\#^1$ (e^{b1} for lower voices).

2. Now have the chorus *sing* a descending scale from a^1-a (8 va for boys) without changing timbres below the $f\#$ transition note. A clear soft tone will be heard on the low pitches. You will hear a sudden increase in volume if any of the singers switch timbres within the last few notes of the scale. Point out the sudden change to the singers and try again.

3. *Singing upper timbres downward: Speak* an *ah* or *ee* siren beginning forte on a^2 and descending to a^1 (octave lower for boys), getting softer as the siren descends. The timbre does not change if the volume decreases sufficiently as the chorus descends below $f\#^2$. Listen again for sudden increases in volume caused by some students changing timbres on the lower notes.

4. Have the chorus sing a descending scale from a^2-a (8va for boys) without changing timbre. (Make pitch adjustments for basses and altos in all the above exercises—speak and sing from f^2-g^1 (octave lower for boys) in exercises 3 and 4).

   Maintaining the timbre below the transition notes implies maintaining the energy level of the upper timbre for the lower pitches. This guarantees a soft tone that has vitality and carrying power. It's still all done by singing in the imagination.

When we speak in the imgination the speech moves up and down in vertical channel—not in a back to front route, but rather in a straight vertical line which extends from the chest to the temples. Picture a profile of yourself and draw a straight line from your temple downward with your hand. This is the route of your aural image with normal variation in front and in back of the line for emotional coloration (brightness and darkness).

Students tend to pull back on low tones. Tell them to think high as they sing downward. This helps them stay inside the anatomy. Conversely, students tend to push forward when they go higher in pitch. Suggesting they think down as they sing higher helps them to stay in the verticle channel.

Start the tone as if you were speaking it, and sing within the vertical alignment of the initial tone. Any attempt to move a tone forward or backward after the attack will cause tension in the vocal mechanism. Remember, voice movement in the imagination depends more on the volume of the speech sound than on the pitch.

Consider a five-note ascending and descending scale in middle timbre, for example. If the singer imagines a crescendo as he goes higher, the imagined tones actually move in opposition to the pitch movement.

Messa Di Voce: The Crescendo-Diminuendo

Seventeenth and eighteenth century *bel canto* treatises on singing emphasize the importance of crescendo-diminuendo exercises and teach that the *messa di voce* is achieved by singing with different registers (timbres) on a single pitch. (See Figure 5-2.) — Note the timbre sequence in Figure 5-2: the tone begins softly; the pitch $\underline{f}^1$ is imagined with upper timbre and crescendoed to the limit of the upper timbre; the singers then switch to middle timbre, which is swelled to its limit; and finally, the singers sing the pitch with chest timbre to reach

Figure 5-2

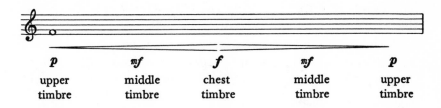

p	**mf**	**f**	**mf**	**p**
upper timbre	middle timbre	chest timbre	middle timbre	upper timbre

maximum volume. (Chest timbre can be sung above $\underline{f}^1$ but authorities agree that it is vocally injurious to do so.) A diminuendo is achieved by reversing the timbre sequence.

Guidelines for Teaching Dynamics:

1. Soft singing results when a pitch is imagined with a higher timbre than the one normally designated.
2. Here is an example of transferring speech to singing in a rehearsal to obtain forte singing. (See Figure 5-3.)

Figure 5-3   **climax of The Falcon Gerrish**

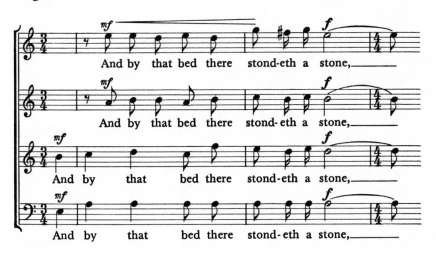

Have each section speak aloud within the pitch of the a minor chord that most closely fits its part—basses a, tenors c^1, altos a^1, sopranos e^2. Speak the whole line in rhythm with up and down inflections. When you are satisfied the chorus is speaking with full-voiced freedom, have the students sing the pitches of the song by imitating their speech sounds, without hesitation or critical judgment. Repeat the process until you are satisfied that the singing sounds the same as the speech. The sopranos will imagine a change from middle timbre to upper timbre on the words "standeth a" and back to middle timbre on "stone." The other voices speak and sing in pure middle timbres. Sing silently, sing aloud, maintaining the ryhthmic pulse between the silent perforamnce and the actual one.

Teaching Vocal Flexibility

Students can sing fast runs as quickly as they can imagine aural images move when they imagine singing the runs silently. Take a florid passage from a choral work you are rehearsing and ask the chorus to sing the passage silently. Start the passage slowly. Repeat the passage several times, quickening the tempo on each repeat. Those singers who can imagine the voice move at a fast tempo can sing aloud at that tempo.

Practicing fast florid passages and scales teaches students to sing intuitively. They do not have time to hesitate between notes or to be critical of the sound of their voices. Make fast florid singing a part of your rehearsals. Practice singing rapid notes silently in the imagination before singing aloud until articulation becomes smooth and clear. Never use the inter-polated h in florid passages. This is physical, and detrimental to mental coordination. The first attempts at fast singing might be awkward and the running notes might sound unarticulated. Keep practicing until the articulation becomes natural. Remind your singers not to think ahead, but rather to imagine each sound the instant they sing it. In other words, stay in rhythm. Imagine each sound within its rhythmic subdivision.

Expression In Singing

We all want our students to sing with expression. We want to hear it in the voice and in the words, and we want to see the effect of emotion on their faces. (I am speaking here about inward emotional response, not interpretation.)

1. Speaking in upper timbres, with the proper inflection of a text, helps students to become sensitive to poetry and the sound of beautiful speech.
2. Singing silently in the imagination helps students to "feel" musical in a way that students might not feel when they sing aloud.
3. I have found the following directives to be helpful in drawing emotional response from singers. "Sing a phrase of a song in your imagination. 'Imagine' the phrase again with appropriate expression. Imagine it again exactly the way you want it to sound. Do it again with more feeling. Now sing aloud, letting the imagined sound guide your voice."

   The addition of emotion to silent singing injects a quality into the singers they did not have before. It's like reading a play to yourself and then acting that same play out on the stage. The magic of art becomes personal. You become a part of it. "Sing aloud, feeling the same emotion you did while singing in the imagination."

Emotional Vitality

Emotion plays an immeasurable part in singing. All artistic singing contains this factor, but emotional vitality is in some ways the most nebulous aspect of teaching to sing. Most teachers achieve emotional vitality through the magnetism of their personalities. I suppose all teachers do to some extent. I have tried to analyze the role inspiration plays in singing, and I have no doubt that emotion which results from inspiration causes the nervous system to work with greater efficiency. The concepts of aural image presented in this book cannot be carried off on an artistic level without individual emotional vitality and involvement.

The process of neurological repatterning is explained in the relatively new claims of the science of psycho-cybernetics: that the thoughts we have in our imagination have as much effect on our nervous system as the things we actually do. Singing in the imagination and trusting the imagination to guide all aspects of the vocal mechanism repatterns the nervous system and enables singers to sing: (1) with freedom, (2) with a full dynamic range, (3) with flexibility, and (4) with true emotion.

Any method you devise which encourages students to sing by their imaginations will have a positive effect on their singing.

Singing with Spirit

Music and intuition (man's spirit) are closely allied. Music is the medium through which man best expresses his spirit from himself to that of another person. How then can we get our students to infuse spirit into the music they are singing?

I believe the imagination is the source for all intuition, and it is in the imagination that man builds his self-image. *What we think, we become.* There is no way to *put* emotion into singing except through that which we imagine. I tell my students to let the imagination do it all, not passively but actively, by their will. The muscles of the body are innervated by the sounds we imagine; the chemical reactions that cause emotions are innervated by the feelings, the energy, and the vitality we imagine while we sing. The greater a singer's capacity to sing in the imagination intuitively (that is, without critical judgment), the greater his ability to communicate his spirit to those who hear him sing.

Teaching Intonation

Poor intonation is a result, not a cause: too much talking about pitch and intonation inhibits choristers and slows up their aural-image process. Therefore, I seldom mention pitch and intonation to my chorus. Wandering minds (poor aural images) and/or tensions which interfere with the working of the vocal mechanism cause poor pitch and intonation. When choristers have learned the notes accurately and *trust* their aural images to guide their vocal mechanisms, intonation is secure.

If the intonation is bad, follow this procedure to find the cause. Conduct the choir as it imagines the composition (or a passage of it) silently. When you reach a cadence, have the choir sing aloud. If they sing the cadence in tune, the former bad intonation was the result of wandering minds, or of not imitating their speech sounds when they were singing. If they will sing the cadence out of tune, flat or sharp, the notes have not been accurately learned. The choristers can tell you exactly where in the music they had trouble imagining pitches. Check all dificult intervals and the thirds and sevenths in the phrase. Drill these notes until tonal membory is complete. Tonal memory is complete when your singers can sing their voice parts clearly in their imaginations. Practice until the chorus can sing the passasage silently and the cadence aloud in tune, on pitch.

Any training that permanently detracts from aural image hurts a student's chances of singing in tune, no matter how much ability he has. A basketball player, when shooting a foul shot, concentrates either on the front rim of the basket or a spot on the hoop. His total concentration must be at that particular spot if he is to be accurate, physically relaxed and coordinated. A good player learns that there is a definite relationship between his ability to relax and his power of concentration. He also learns he is incompetent as a scorer when he thinks about his muscles or his form.

The baseball batter keeps his eyes on the ball from the instant it leaves the pitcher's hand. Any mental deviation from the pitched ball will cause tightness and lack of coordination in the body. The player who gets in a batting slump often tries a new batting stance or holds the bat differently, but it is not until he regains confidence to concentrate wholly on the ball that he again starts hitting.

Instrumentalists are more prone to consciously guide muscles by imagining pitches than singers are. The trumpet player, for instance, never attempts to consciously adjust lip tension for each pitch: he imagines a pitch and then plays, letting the muscles of the body and lips react.

Clarinetists and flutists couldn't possibly be conscious of lifting their fingers up and down on fast passages. They imagine pitches and away the fingers go. Singers who learn these principles gain confidence that their instruments respond to mental innervation also. This concept is paramount to singers if they are going to learn to sing in tune with freedom.

Psychological Aspects of Intonation

People can't learn when they are constantly being told they can't. A study conducted at the Oak School in San Francisco shows that if teacher expectancy of pupils' intellectual growth is raised, startling improvement can be achieved in pupils' IQ within eight months. Another study conducted at a high school in New Jersey revealed that some pupils fail because teachers thought they were less intelligent than IQ tests later indicated.[1]

Voice teachers and choral directors place unnecessary talent limitations on their students. Every student has musical and vocal gifts (barring those who have physical and mental handicaps) which can be developed. I have known "monotones" who have learned to sing in tune by first understanding the role

---

1. "Studies Cite Causes of Success and Failure", *Ohio Schools* (pub. by the Ohio State Education Association), Dec., 1967, p. 8.

the imagination has in singing, and then by gaining confidence in themselves through rehearsal.

Self-Motivation

Inner drive and self-confidence are important for a student to change his vocal habits and realize improvement. Self-motivation results when people sense "worth" within themselves. How can we help students realize their musical worth (potential)?

First, give positive directions. Positive directions encourage weak singers to trust their imagined pitch and speech images while they improve their concepts of speech timbres. Telling students they are flat or sharp breaks down confidence in aural image; the students revert to physical tension and the choristers begin to "tune up" to those around, always singing late and light. When your choral singers trust their images they become exciting members of your choral group. If images are not right, it's our job to improve them through speaking by aural image, silent practice, and anything else that will help students trust their imaginations to guide their voices.

Just as you are not negative in your criticism, discourage your singers from being negative in self-criticism. Singing in the imagination can be explained *logically* but must be harnessed *intuitively*. One cannot judge himself critically and produce clear, beautiful singing. Teach the student how he guides his voice by aural image and then encourage him to act upon his aural images without reservation.

This whole psychological process in trusting the imagined sound implies that, if necessary, we allow our students to sing out of tune in the beginning stages of learning how to sing. We must keep our goals in front of us. As the singers gain confidence in their aural image technique, intonation improves. A conductor who constantly tells his chorus they are flat ends up with a group of students too inhibited to sing and who eventually lose the enjoyment they originally found in singing.

Guidelines:

1. Poor intonation caused by lack of mental concentration can be helped through silent practice.
2. Imitating the correct speech timbre with each pitch is an important aspect of improving intonation.
3. Keep the mention of intonation to a minimum except while pointing out incorrect notes, and progress toward good intonation.
4. Use the *silent singing technique* to determine if the notes are thoroughly learned.
5. Encourage your singers to believe in their speech sounds.
6. Be positive in your directions.

Spinning Tone

A good tone spins (true vibrato); a bad tone is either straight (no vibrato) or wavy (slow vibrato). Spin results when pitch and speech timbres are imitated exactly when singing, and when the energy in the imagination of the sung tones matches the imagined energy of the speech sounds. The lengthening, shortening, and thickening of vocal folds result from images sent to the laryngeal muscles by way of nerves. Nerves shoot back and forth from the brain to the pitch-regulating muscles, causing a pulsation which in turn causes a recurring pitch variation known as vibrato. A vibrato is correct when (1) the muscles in the larynx are innervated by imagined pitch and speech sounds, and (2) when the larynx is free from extrinsic muscular interference.

I describe vibrato as "spin" rather than a wave ⌢⌣⌢ because it is closer to what singers experience when their voices sing freely. Most authorities agree that a true vibrato pulsates between six and seven times per second. A straight tone, a wavy tone (a slow vibrato) and tremolo (vibrato of excessive speed) are caused by tensions in the larynx resulting from uncoordinated aural images and/or excessive physical energy. Sometimes singers cannot free extrinsic muscles of the larynx even when aural image concepts are being established because neurological patterns of tension have been already formed. The spinning technique outlined below helps overcome patterns of tension and helps develop the aural concept of free-spining vibrato.

Spinning Gesture

Stand with good posture. At chest level, make a small, fast, forward, circular motion with your dominant hand. Let your body muscles bounce as you spin your hand. Sustain a spoken "nah" or "nee" siren as you spin. Notice how the tone bounces (the more bounce the better).

Have the whole choir sing on "nah" while they spin. The key is to let the voices bounce. Tell the singers to actually feel the bounce inside—spin fast and vigorously—but without tension. You can motivate students to let the voice spin by demonstrating a free-spinning tone, a wavy tone, and a straight tone. If you cannot demonstrate these, use students who can.

Spinning, when done with speed, energy, and released muscles, brings with it a sudden surge of free tone from a chorus. The voices resonate in the free and open pharyngeal areas of the singers' throats. The larynges are released from their abnormal high positions (normal for most untrained singers) and the pharynx walls are released—two important contributors to resonant singing.

What Does Spinning Do?

(1) Spinning releases extrinsic muscles that usually interfere with the innervated muscles of the vocal mechanism, (2) it teaches vitality because of the increased physical activity, (3) it gives confidence to the choristers, (4) it helps develop a concept of free-spinning vibrato, (5) it overcomes any reluctance to let

the vibrato into the voice, and (6) it gives a psychological lift to a rehearsal because of the physical activity and the big sound that results.

Spinning doesn't work when (1) the singers spin too slowly, (2) the singers hold their muscles (stomach, shoulders, chest or neck) rigid, (3) the singers' spinning circle is too large, (4) the singers resist the vocal "bouncing" that results from the spin, and (5) the singers fail to concentrate on their aural images while they spin.

When To Use Spinning Technique

Spinning can be done any time during a rehearsal or lesson to obtain freedom or merely to revitalize the rehearsal. Use the spinning gesture on music that is memorized. Teach spinning tone as imagery. For legato singing and smooth line, the singers must let the voice spin all the time. Each word spins into the next. The technique of popular singers which sounds ⎯⌇⌇⌇⌇⌇⌇ on each word seems to influence even some "artist singers." The ideal phrase is one in which spin never stops. Remember, a free voice spins naturally. Straight tone and slow vibratos result from tense muscles.

Choral Blend

Choral blend results when all the singers in the chorus imagine pitch images with pure speech timbres and correct vowels. For example, if all the sopranos sing *ah* on a^1 with pure middle timbre, the voices blend. There is no need for special blending such as listening to each other, matching vibratos, or any other artifical blending technique. A soloist who guides the voice by sining in the imagination makes a good chorister. Tell your singers *not* to listen to each other. Tell them to concentrate on sining in their imagination and aloud simultaneously.

It is difficult enough to sing by the imagination without the necessity of listening to those around you to hear if *they* are right or wrong. Tell your singers to sing as though they were all separated in sound-proof booths, each person doing "his own thing." A quartet chorus arrangement or a scrambled arrangement where no two persons from any one section are next to each other helps singers gain this kind of independence.

The two most important aspects of blend are vowels and timbre. Your blend problems are solved once your singers can imagine pure vowels in correct timbres, and when they sing without hestitation or critical judgment. Singing this way is fun, and helps singers become independent and secure musicians.

CHAPTER 6

Teaching Breathing in the High School Chorus

To SOME TEACHERS, diaphragmatic breathing holds the key to good singing. The preceding chapters explain how the muscles used in singing are cortically regulated and neurologically stimulated by the imagination. These muscles used in singing include those indispensable to respiration. Without breath flowing past the vibrating vocal folds, there is no voice. Breath carries the vibrations initiated in the larynx to the resonators, and most authorities believe breath causes vocal fold vibration in some way or another.

Theories of Vocal Fold Vibration

There are many theories of vocal fold vibration. The classic theory says breath builds up in the glottis and forces the preadjusted vocal folds into vibration, which in turn releases puffs of vibrated air which are then resonated above the larynx. Vennard presents a theory called the Bernoulli effect, which claims the breath in the glottis works as suction which sucks the folds into vibration before they fully close: "First the flow of breath sucks the glottis shut; this stops the flow momentarily, whereupon breath pressure blows the glottis open again; air flow recommences and the cycle repeats."[1] A third theory advocated by Raoul Husson claims the folds are neurologically vibrated; that is, vibration of vocal folds results from nerve impulses sent by the brain. According to this authority nerve impulses are sent from the brain to the larynx, vocal fold vibration begins, and the breath resonates the tone in the larynx and the superior cavities.

Which theory, if any, will prove true, I do not know. In Husson's theory, breath pressure has nothing to do with vibration. The Bernoulli effect emphasizes that breath force against the vocal folds for vibration is necessary.

The emphasis on breath pressure for vocal power has been overstated. One neurological process governs respiration as well as phonation more than we were once willing to accept.

This chapter discusses neuro-physiological aspects of breathing and how to adapt them to breath teaching procedures. Some excellent recent publications outline technical aspects of neuro-physiology in respiration; few of them present practical application of their technical discussions for singers. This chapter attempts to fill this void. I remind you at the outset that breathing supplements singing by aural image, and should be taught only in addition to mental control concepts of vocal production.

Breath Control Misconceptions

Many advocates of the "breath control" singing school strive for some form of "super-normal" breathing. Although abnormal breathing can be detrimental to coordination in singing, there is no such thing as super-normal breathing; there is no method of breathing that in itself makes us sing well. Normal breathing

---

1. William Vennard, *Singing: The Mechanism and the Technic* p. 42.

helps; abnormal breathing hinders. Tensing the stomach organs against the diaphragm, holding the rib cage open, pushing down with the shoulders, balancing chest pressure against stomach pressure, or breathing in the lower abdomen may be considered by some as super-normal, but these techniques are in reality abnormalities to the breathing cycle.

Some Important Scientific Findings About Breathing

The method of teaching breathing in this chapter rests upon the following neuro-physiological principles:

1. All speech and singing involves control of the breathing apparatus in the imagination.

2. When the lungs are emptied of breath the diaphragm is innervated; it then pushes down and opens the rib cage (thorax). By reverse innervation it lifts up and closes the rib cage; that is, after the lungs are filled.

3. Breath *force* is not the main factor in the crescendo and diminuendo of volume. The fraction of the cycle time that the cords remain closed is the main physical factor in determining the volume. This time element is determined by the loudness and softness of the speech timbre.

4. After one inhales, a reflex action causes him to exhale. This action is involuntary. The strength of diaphragmatic reflexes depends on the degree to which our lungs are expanded during breath intake and, conversely, on the extent to which our lungs are collapsed after expiration.

5. Carrying power, resonance, and vocal color do not depend on the type of breathing (diaphragmatic, intercostal, or clavicular) or upon lung capacity. When singers imagine good speech and pitch images and trust them, they discover the key to carrying power and resonance.

6. Breath functions as a part of the whole. Singing is a coordination of phonation, respiration, articulation, and resonation, but the coordination of these separate aspects into one

function is achieved in the imagination. These scientific findings show that breath is neurologically controlled, and that the concept of breath as the most important aspect of singing is mythology.

Unnatural Breathing

Involuntary breathing is cortically controlled. Nevertheless, the influence of breathing by direct voluntary means is possible and for some singers habitual. Tensing the stomach muscles, compressing the chest against a tightened abdomen wall, etc., are learned actions (either consciously or unconsciously). If such "voluntary" controls are habit, the student experiences much frustration when he tries to sing by neurological control (letting the breath follow mental thought).

Natural Breathing

The singer who is unspoiled, who has not learned a mechanical approach to breathing, can learn correct breathing in a relatively short time. I use "correct breathing" rather than abdominal or intercostal because the placement of an involuntary breath into the body during a neurological inspiration depends particularly upon a person's sex. Kaplan makes this very clear to us: " . . . abdominal or diaphragmatic breathing characterizes the male. It is in contrast with a type called costal or rib breathing which characterizes the female. Teleologically explained, the action at a higher level is an adaptation to prevent undue pressure on a rising uterus in the gravid female."[2] In other words, breathing too low is unnatural for the female because of her created purpose of child bearing. My own research has proven the above differences between male and female are true. One can force abdominal breathing on girls, but

2. Harold M. Kaplan, *Anatomy and Physiology of Speech,* (New York: McGraw-Hill Book Co., Inc., 1960), p. 88.

all who learn to breathe according to the steps below are assured correct expansion of the body and consequently the correct filling of the lungs.

Directions For Correct Respiration

1. Blow out all the breath from your lungs that you can (muscles must not become tense). Maintain good posture.
2. Let your thorax open and let the breath enter silently (but rapidly through a relaxed throat).
3. Release the breath muscles as you sustain the tone.

Step 1. Blow out all your breath. Without tensing, exhale as much breath as you can. Remember the emptier your lungs, the stronger the reflex action of the diaphragm and thorax. To prove to yourself that the diaphragm and thorax are innervated and do not need extrinsic control, place one hand across your lower rib cage and waist, empty the lungs of air, and feel the expansion of your thorax and the waist line without inhaling. Of course, any tension in the body interferes with the free action of the innervated muscles. After a student has experienced the diaphragm reflex, he beings to understand the part innervation plays in respiration and how "voluntary" control (tension) hinders respiration. Langley and Cheraskin write: "The only reason air moves into the lungs during inspiration is because the pressure within the lungs is lower than the pressure of the outside air. The lungs and chest do not expand because of the entry of air, it is just the other way around. Air moves in because the chest and lungs expand."[3] We can change this by voluntary control, but we can't improve on it.

Step 2. Breathe silently. Since breath moves into the lungs automatically when the pressure inside is less than the pressure outside, we don't have to inhale breath by muscular pull.

---

3. Leroy Langley and E. Cheraskin, *Physiology of Man* (New York: Reinhold Publishing Co. 1965), p. 358.

However, if our stomach organs are tight at the end of a previous expiration, the innervated diaphragm cannot move down and the thorax will not open. The space for inspiration is cramped. Imagine the organs of your stomach stiffened against the diaphragm. If these organs are rigid, the diaphragm cannot open the thorax neurologically. The incoming air has no place to go but into the upper chest and neck area. Correct breath is impossible no matter how low we try to force our breath. The stomach muscles must be released before the breath cycle can be correct.

As soon as the muscles are released, the thorax opens. When this act is followed by a silent breath, correct inspiration is assured; more abdominal in the male, more intercostal in the female. Deep inspiration should be automatic—tense stomach muscles prevent deep inspiration.

The Silent Breath: A silent inspiration of breath helps singers four ways: (1) it avoids neck tension (pulling the breath in by sucking or gaspong causes tight neck muscles); (2) it releases the singers both physiologically and psychologically; (3) it helps to keep the stomach muscles from tensing; and (4) it permits the breath to fill the lungs according to each singer's individual sex and posture peculiarities.

How do many successful singers who have become voice instructors teach? They analyze their posture and how they breathe, and advocate their way for everyone, regardless of sex or build. This "conform to the way I do it" attitude frustrates many, helping only those who happen to fit the teacher's physical mold. The automatic silent breath determines the type of breathing (more abdominal in some, more costal in others) best suited for each singer. High chest and shoulder breathing never results when directions one and two govern inspiration.

Teaching the Diaphragm To Open and Close the Thorax

At first, students have trouble inhaling quickly and silently.

Imagine breathing at different rates of speed. Practice opening the thorax rapidly by cortical control (without breath). Here's how: Blow the breath out, hold your mouth closed, and shut off the nasal passages with a thumb and forefinger. With your other hand, feel the thorax jump open (stomach muscles must not be tense). Open the mouth and let the breath rush in. This process teaches your body how to release breath so the diaphragm can make thorax adjustments. Once your body knows experientially that the diaphragm, thorax and flow of air operate neurophysiologically, body tension begins to subside.

Long and short breaths should be silent, through a relaxed throat, into an innervated open thorax. Long breaths should be through the nose to help prevent the breath from drying the throat. Short, quick breaths must be through the open mouth. In either case your breath should be as noiseless as possible.

A noisy breath invariably tenses the muscles of the neck, drys the throat and places the breath into the wrong places of the body; that is, in the neck, the shoulder areas, or too low in the stomach. Breath incorrectly placed requires muscle tension to force the breath back out. The whole neurophysiological process is destroyed.

Releasing the Breath

The loud-sigh explained in Chapter One teaches singers how to release breath without tension. Singing with the same energy as speech in the imagination teaches students how to release breath without tensing muscles while they sing. Singing requires mental energy. We imagine the same energy when we sing as when we speak.

Some singers mistakenly think tensing the abdomen wall helps support the outflow of air. Actually, tense body muscles inhibit support. Body tension holds the breath inside the lungs.

How To Check Your Singers' Breath Release

Have them blow out their air and inhale silently; sustain a tone as long as they can; exhale at the end of the tone. If singers blow out breath when they feel the air is depleted, you know excessive body tension existed and some air was not allowed out during the sung tone. A very tense singer often exhales a surprisingly large volume of air at the end of a tone. On the other hand, poor phonation (poor muscular coordination in the larynx) allows excessive breath to escape at the outset of tone, which seriously hampers the singer's ability to sustain a long tone. When inspiration is correct as previously outlined, the causes of breath shortage are either excessive air escaping when the tone begins, or breath remains imprisoned in the lungs because of body tension.

Briefly: Evidence shows that volume and carrying power of a sung tone depend on the coordinated action within the larynx (phonation) and the effect of the resonators upon the sound waves—not the type of respiration or vital capacity of the lungs. No "super-normal" pressure helps; all necessary muscles are controlled in the imagination and stimulated by nerves. When one imagines more volume and/or higher pitches, the needed respiratory muscles are set in action. Practice singing in the imagination letting the mouth move as if singing aloud. Coordinate the breath cycle with the imagined singing. Inhale silently; release the breath as you sing in the imagination. Breathe in the appropriate musical places. Continue the process throughout an entire musical composition until the choristers experience the natural innervation of the respiratory system. Then sing aloud, letting the imagination guide the whole vocal mechanism.

Guidelines

1. Without tension, blow out all the air you can.

2. Let the thorax relax and open.

3. Breathe in silently (100 percent noiselessly).

4. Men expand more abdominally, women more intercostally.

5. Sustain tone in the imagination without tensing the body. Stop singing when you feel tension mounting.

6. Blow out to see that no air has been held in the lungs.

7. Let the thorax open and the breath come in silently but rapidly through a relaxed throat; go through the process again.

8. The breath cycle is: Muscles released, lungs emptied; silent inspiration; released expiration cortically controlled. If you have several rehearsals a week, this breath cycle can be taught in a relatively short period. By the second semester silent breathing should be automatic.

9. The only conscious act in the whole breathing cycle is the silent inspiration—any conscious effort beyond this hampers the natural coordination of the breath muscles and their neuro-glandular control.

10. Singing requires the same physical energy as speaking in the tessitura of the singing. The energy level is controlled by imitating speech when singing.

11. Physical control inhibits; mental control frees.

Conducting the Breath

A conductor's preparatory beat signifies the rate of inspiration, tempo, dynamic level, and style (legato, staccato, etc.). Most conductors breathe with their choirs. If you gasp in a breath, the choristers will gasp; if you inhale silently, so will the choir (once they have been taught to do so). A tense arm and preparation signals a tense breath; a jerky preparation, a jerky breath. Be careful to use free-flowing preparations, no matter what style ensues, until the choir has good habits of inspiration.

Breathe-sing: never stop or hold the breath before you sing. The preparation should signal the singers to start singing the instant the lungs are full. Never delay starting the tone once the preparation is given.

Staggered Breathing

Staggered breathing is a technique whereby a choir can sing longer phrases than individuals in the choir can. Silent catch breaths are taken on the vowels and, when possible, on long notes; a word should never be cut short, as this destroys the precision of the consonants. Direct your singers to breathe as often as they wish, breathing on vowels (not between words) and silently. Staggered breathing helps your beginning singers maintain physical release if they are reminded to breath often and silently (think the breath in), and are admonished to "never sing when you are running out of breath."

Staggered breathing can be free (breath any place you want), or formal (all those with last names beginning with A through F breathe on first beats only; G-L, breathe on second beats; M-R on third beats, and S-Z on fourth beats). Henry Coward explained a very effective use of this technique on long runs such as those found in Handel's *Messiah*.[4]

Breathiness

Although the cause of breathiness has little to do with respiration as such, I feel a discussion of it is appropriate here. Phonation involves many more muscles and cartilages than the vocal folds alone. The imbalance of the muscle tensions within the larynx allows excessive breath to escape; breathy tone results. The problem of muscular imbalance is solved when students learn to transfer clear speech to singing. Be sure your students use the same mental energy when they sing as when they speak. Breathiness disappears when pitch is imagined with free speech in the correct register. It is futile to try to overcome breathiness by working on breathing exercises.

4. Henry Coward, *Choral Technique and Interpretation* (New York: H.W. Gray Co.), p. 213.

Posture

Standing or sitting with minimum strain on your body so your organs have room to function efficiently is good posture.

A tense body is a weak body. To illustrate this, ask a husky boy to lift one end of a piano while he tenses his stomach muscles and holds his breath. He can succeed only with much effort and strain. Then have him lift without tensing, flexing upward from the level of the hips (the balance level) without holding his breath. The results are always surprising. (I have done this at high school choir festivals—a *strong* volunteer is always easy to find.)

Misconceptions of good posture include: (1) a high chest supported by tense back and neck muscles, and (2) a flattened stomach accomplished by tensing the abdominal wall. The results look good but the person feels terrible. The tension in the stomach prevents the innervated diaphragm from opening the thorax, and the resultant breath is too high. Swayback, another detrimental body position, prevents the diaphragm from expanding at the sides and back—belly breathing results. Some singers hold the rib cage open to make room for the breath to come in. I have already shown that this is unscientific. Besides, singers who consciously hold their rib cage out do so with tight stomach muscles, which inhibit the breath intake.

Checking Your Students' Posture

Students who have learned to breathe by the silent breath method can check their posture by noting where the body expands during inspiration.

1. When the stomach expands but not the sides or back, it is because they are standing too swayed.
2. When the upper chest expands and not the waist, it is because their stomach muscles are pulled in and the diaphragm cannot function.

3. When they expand primarily in the back, it is because their shoulders are pulled down and tensed.

The three goals in posture are: a slightly elevated chest position, a flattened stomach wall that is not tense, and as little sway in the back and neck as possible without tension or loss of balance (some persons have more natural sway than others).

How To Maintain Good Standing Posture

Balance in posture is important to neural health and deep breathing. The hips are the normal horizontal balance point for good posture. (See Figure 6-1.)

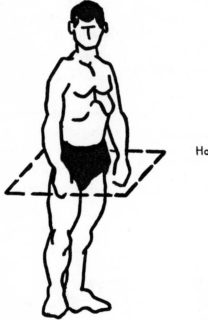

Figure 6-1

Horizontal plane of the body

Drawing of a figure with horizontal plane of the body.

Teach your students to balance their bodies on the horizontal plane to achieve a lifted position. In a collapsed posture, one foot slightly ahead of the other, place your hands on your hips with the index fingers on the hip bone. Turn your hips slightly down and under, and simultaneously lift the torso upward and forward. (See Figure 6-2.)

Figure 6-2

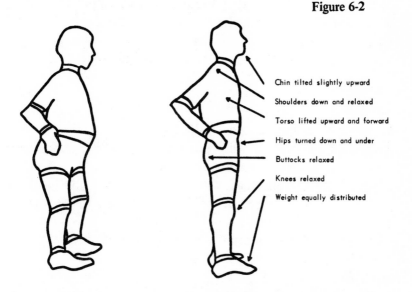

Chin tilted slightly upward

Shoulders down and relaxed

Torso lifted upward and forward

Hips turned down and under

Buttocks relaxed

Knees relaxed

Weight equally distributed

Drawing of two standing figures pointing out proper posture.

The hips and torso move easily, as one, into a comfortable, lifted position. This posture causes the abdominal wall to flatten and the chest to elevate. (Too much chest elevation makes a person look like a pigeon, or at best a stuffed shirt.) At the end of the gesture, distribute the body weight evenly on your feet (neither on the heels nor on the toes). The posture movement can and should be done without tensing the buttocks. Shoulders are relaxed and down, and the knees unlocked. Think of the movement as a ballet gesture—one movement operates all the individual muscles. Significantly, no thought is given to specific parts of the body; attention to specific muscles is psychologically inhibiting; do the whole gesture and let the parts fall into place. Comfort determines the extent of the movement.

Posture adjustments should be made a little at a time rather than all at once. Too much change causes awkwardness and defeats students before they begin. (Until the improved posture feels natural, it burdens the singer rather than helps.) Remind your students how opera singers manage beautiful singing in all kinds of positions. Their skill is mental, not physical.

Guidelines:

1. Posture influences physical, mental and neural health. Organs work efficiently when posture is not tense.
2. A good appearance results from good posture.
3. Good posture must become habit so it doesn't interfere with the mental concentration necessary for neurophysiological coordination.
4. Good posture results when the body is lifted and maintained from the level of the hips. All lifting strength comes from the hip level.
5. Tense muscles are weak muscles. Only when the abdomen and intercostal muscles are released can diaphragm and thorax function efficiently.
6. Lifted posture is achieved by turning the hips down and under, and simultaneously lifting the torso upward and forward. A mirror can help judge the extent of movement, but comfort is the first consideration—any tension in the buttocks, abdomen or chest muscles indicates overdoing the movement.
7. Posture like breathing supplements aural image, and its importance should not get out of line of the true cause of singing. Teach breathing and posture after the students know experiencially how the imagination controls singing.

How To Maintain Good Seated Posture

The same principles of maintaining a free lift in the body at the level of the hips can be applied to seated posture. Push the hips backward while the torso is lifted slightly upward and forward. (See Figure 6-3.)

Figure 6-3

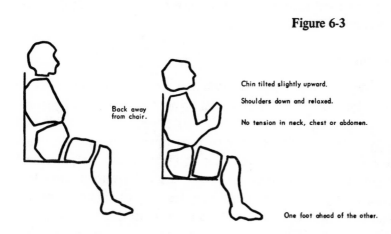

Back away from chair.

Chin tilted slightly upward.

Shoulders down and relaxed.

No tension in neck, chest or abdomen.

One foot ahead of the other.

Drawing of two seated figures pointing out proper posture.

This is the same position one takes just before standing. The lift is felt only at the hip level, just as in the standing position. Comfort determines the extent of the movement.

Singers and choirs stand in performances; rehearsals prepare for performance; therefore practices should be done mostly in standing posture. Chairs are not needed for short rehearsals (less than fifty minutes) except in the beginning of a school year. Practicing correct seated posture, however, can teach your students how to lift from the level of the hips. In both seated and standing postures the body should be free to swivel from side to side; the singer should feel buoyant.

How To Stand From a Seated Position

The scraping of chairs when a seated choir rises to sing after a beautiful solo in a cantata or oratorio annoys any conductor. This can be corrected easily: first, establish correct seated posture—right foot slightly ahead of left foot, backs away from chairs; then push the body straight up by the heel of the right foot and the ball of the left foot; after a few practices the noisy movement of chairs will disappear.

Calisthenics

After a student has spent a few hours in study and class recitations, a choir rehearsal can be both relaxing and invigorating to him. *The National Football League Guide to Physical Fitness* states: "The essense of relaxation is change. Man must have variety in his life in order to maintain his zest, alertness, and optimistic outlook."[5] (This is a good argument for daily choral rehearsals.) A few minutes of calisthenics at the beginning of each rehearsal can be most helpful to music students, physically and psychologically. Young people love exercise and after sitting in a classroom all day, calisthenics are a welcome and healthy change before getting back to mental concentration.

Below are a few calisthenics adaptable to choir rehearsal situations. All can be done in a minimum amount of space, in street clothes, and without embarrassment to anyone.

1. jumping jacks—10 repetitions
2. running in place—20 to 30 seconds
   Start *andante, accelarando* to *allegro* and *ritard* to *andante.*
3. side benders—8 repetitions
4. touching toes—5 to 15 repetitions
   a. do rhythmically
   b. start with 5 per rehearsal and gradually increase to 15

---

5. Richard Pickens, ed. *The National Football Guide to Physical Fitness,* 1965, p. 181.

5. neck flex—3 to 6 repetitions in each position
   Bend the neck forward and try to touch chin to the chest in a bouncing motion. Repeat to the right and left and backward.

Isometrics:

1. push hands together 5 to 10 seconds
   a. at level of stomach
   b. at level of chest
   c. behind the back
2. push left hand down against a raised left knee 5 to 10 seconds
   Switch to right hand and knee.
3. pull hands apart
   Same as number 1

Run in place or do jumping jacks at the end of isometric exercises to relax all muscles.

These are only a few possibilities to get your started.

Emphasize the importance of good diet and adequate sleep to your choir. Your students' health needs attention if the nerves, muscles, and organs are to be efficient in singing. An individual calisthenic regimen including push-ups, leg-ups, knee bends, etc., can supplement the calisthenics done in rehearsals. Choral rehearsals can be many things: a period of mental discipline, a time of body building, a place to improve breathing habits and improve one's health and appearance, a time to learn to sing and learn new music, a time for social integration, and a period to grow esthetically and spiritually. These are pretty good reasons for having chorus in the curriculum.

CHAPTER 7

Obtaining Good Diction in Voice

Training

GOOD DICTION INCLUDES correct pronunciation, clear enunciation and free articulation—correct vowels and consonants sung with clarity and proper inflection, and with free muscular movements.

Your voice quality (speech timbre) depends on your vibrator and resonance cavities. Your speech images determine the quality and beauty of your vocal timbre. What vowels and consonants you imagine determine the action of your articulators. Clear diction depends on the correct action of the articulation system.

How To Get Good Diction

Music enhances the text. If words aren't clear to the listener, he is left to surmise what has been sung and has heard only half of the composition. Intelligent presentations of texts include:

1. correct vowels
2. rhythmic articulation of diphthongs
3. precise consonants

4. consonant stress relative to word sense and emotional impact
5. natural word accents
6. key sentence words stressed
7. word connections and separations depending on style and word sense.

Pure Vowels And Corresponding Symbols

	International Phonetic Alphabet	*Dictionary Symbols*
ah as in father, lot	[ɑ]	ä o
a as in vacation, chaos	[e]	ā̲
a as in glad	[ae]	a ă
aw as in all, orb, bought	[ɔ]	ô
ee as in see	[i]	ē
eh as in let	[ɛ]	e ĕ
i as in it	[ɪ]	i ĭ
o as in notation	[o]	o
er as in learn	[3]	ûr ər
ooh as in super, prune	[u]	o͞o
ooh as in good, put	[ʊ]	o͝o
uh as in supper, up, under	[ʌ]	u
closed uh as in ago, sofa	[ə]	ə

agent
sanity
consider
circus

These are all neutral vowels. Some dictionaries distinguish between the neutral a, e, i, o, and u. Others use the [ə] symbol for all of them. I use the [ə] symbol throughout this chapter.

Rules For Singing Vowels

1. Do not make vowels into diphthongs.

2. Sing each vowel in the imagination and aloud simultaneously, and sustain the vowel in the imagination.

3. Know the exact sound of every vowel in a composition. Listen for any deviations from your standard.

4. Teach vowels by imitation. Speech quality should not be imitated, but vowels can be. It's fun and helpful to have your choristers imitate each other's vowel sounds.

5. Stress mental control of vowel sounds.

6. Vowels modify on high pitches because of the excess overtones. However, do not change your image of a vowel on a high pitch unless you do it intentionally to establish upper timbres. The truer the mental concept, the truer the sung vowel will be.

7. Avoid changing agent (aǵ[ə]nt) to a-g[ɛ]nt́: sing either a-́g[ə]nt or a-́g[ɪ]nt.

Briefly, avoid all distortions and affectations. Follow the pronunciation of a good dictionary. Your ear and musical taste must make the final decisions.

Diphthongs And Corresponding Symbols

A diphthong has two vowel sounds in one syllable.

	International Phonetic Alphabet	Dictionary Symbols
i as in time	[ae]	i
a as in say, gay	[eɪ]	a
o as in so, sew	[ou]	o
oi as in toy, boil	[ɔɪ]	oi
ow as in sound, how	[au]	au

Rules:

1. Never break between the two sounds. The connection of one sound to the next is always smooth.

2. Sustain the first vowel. Add the second sound at the end of the syllable. (See Figure 7-1.)

Figure 7-1

night - time   *sing.* n[a]   -   [i] - t[a]   - [i]m

3. Do not accent the second sound.
4. Sing the first vowel sound until the very end of the word, both in florid passages and where there are two or more notes per diphthong.
5. i, a, and oi end in the [I] sound (as in it), not [i] (ee̅); ow and o end in [U] (as in book), not [u] (ooh).
6. Distinguish [e] from [eI]. [e] is the unaccented a as in vacation. It is not diphthongized. Also distinguish [eI] from [εI].

The Neutral Vowel [ə]

The neutral vowels need special attention. The neutral vowel [ə] as in ago, etc., is always found on unaccented syllables. In speech, [ʌ] as in up is the accented *uh* sound; [ə] is the unaccented *uh* sound. Opening the [ə] vowel to [ʌ], [I], [ε] or [ɔ] sometimes causes misplaced accents, which result in affectations and changes in the meaning of the words. For example, ang[ə]l becomes ang[ε]l´ (an affectation); dearest-dear´[ə]st becomes dear-r[ε]st́. Madeleine Marshall writes:

"The principle of non-stress of unaccented syllables by means of the neutral vowel is an integral part of the English language. Without it, there can be no fluent, natural, and effective speaking or singing of English."[1]

---

1. Madeleine Marshall, *The Singer's Manual of English Diction* (New York: G. Schirmer, 1953), p. 153.

Rules for the Neutral Vowel

1. Teach your chorus to sing the [ə] vowel.
2. Always use [ə], when indicated, on short, fast notes. Exception: "beautifully," written in dictionaries as beau-t[ə]-ful, sounds better sung beau-t[I]-ful.
3. Modify (open) neutral vowels on sustained notes only if the meaning of the words does not change. When you modify any vowel, open it to its nearest relative.

closed vowels	*medium vowels*	*open vowels*
[ə] [ɜ]	[ʌ][ɪ][ɛ]	[ɔ][ɑ]

Diphthong Errors and Solutions

Singers make three common mistakes when they sing diphthongs: (1) They change to the second sound too soon, (2) they cause an intermittent third sound by imagining the second vowel too slowly (for example, sound becomes sah-o͞o-und), and (3) they omit the second vowel; shout sounds sh[ɑ]t (shot) rather than sh[ɑ]-o͝ot.

Practice speaking words containing diphthongs in rhythm. Sustain the first vowel and change to the second sound just before the release. (See Figure 7-2.)

Figure 7-2

O praise the Lord all ye na - tions.

Should be sung:

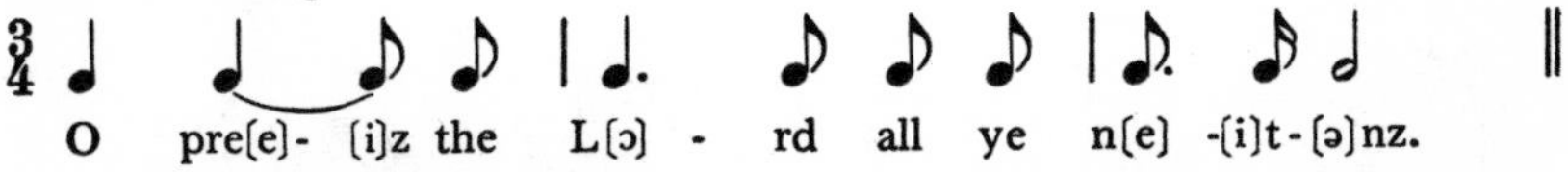

O pre[e]- [i]z the L[ɔ] - rd all ye n[e] -[i]t-[ə]nz.

The rhythmic treatment above can be simplifed by drawing dashes to indicate the proper relationships of the two sounds in a diphthong. Use a pointer at a chalkboard. Drill until word-inflections are correct.

O pre [e]- [i]z the L[ɔ] - rd all' ye n[e] - [i]t -[ə]nz.

The Backward Diphthong

	IPA	Dictionary
<u>yooh</u> as in be<u>au</u>ty, <u>pu</u>re, c<u>u</u>re, m<u>u</u>sic	[ju̯] [iu̯]	u

Rules:

1. Never sing [i̇́] for [ɪ] (as in it) on the initial sound; pure should be sung pih-oohŕ, not peé-oohr.
2. Go immediately to the second sound.
3. Never accent the initial vowel.

R's and Diphthongs

When not correctly articulated, r's make diphthongs out of vowels and triphthongs out of diphthongs:

air should be sung [e]-[ər], not [e]-[ə]-r.
sour   should   be   sung   s[ɑ]-[u̯][ər],   not s[ɑ]-[u̯]-[ə]-r.

I analyzed the text in Figure 7-3 to point up typical vowel and diphthong problems and solutions.

Soprano part from <u>My Shepherd Will Supply My Need</u>

Isaac Watts

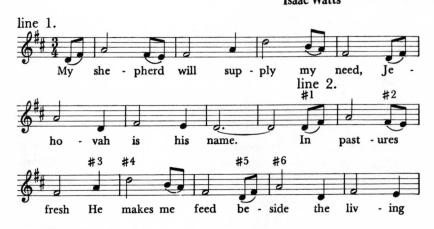

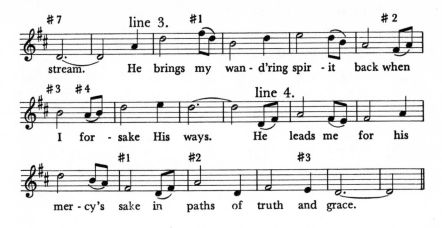

Figure 7-3

Analysis of *My Shepherd Will Supply My Need* (Figure 7-3).

Line 1.

1. Sing M[ɑ́]-[ɪ] shepherd, not mah-eē' shepherd. Don't change to the second sound until after the pitch f has been sung.

2. Omit the "r." Sing sh[ɛ]ph[3]d, not sh[ɛ]ph[ə]rd. Never sing sh[ɛ]-ph[ɑ]rd.

3. Sing [ə], not [ʌ].

4. Sing pl[ɑ]-[ɪ], not pl[ɑ]-[i] plah-ee.

5. Sing J[ɪ], not J[ʌ].

6. Sing h[ɔɯ] (ho-ŏoh), not h[ɔ][ɯ] (ho-ōoh).

7. Sing the [ɪ] with the m, not an instant sooner; n[e]'-[ɪ]m. However, be sure the [ɪ] is heard or the word might sound n[ɛ]m (nehm).

Line 2.

1. Sing (ture) as [3] in fur.

2. [ɪ] as in it, not [i] eē. Notice the correct inflection remains in the word when [ɪ] is articulated.

3. Be sure [ɪ] is heard in the diphthong or the word sounds be-s[ɑ]d.

4. Sing th[ə], not th[ʌ].

Line 3.

1. Be sure the [a e] sound is not nasalized. Imitate your speech when you sing. Do not sing b [ɑ] ck.
2. For can be sung f[ɔ]r and f[ə]r. Sing f[ə]r only on very short notes. On long notes, the open [ɔ] can be sung without changing the natural word inflection.
3. Sing [ɪ]z the instant of release, but be sure the [ɪ] sounds. Otherwise the word sounds w [ɛ] z rather than w [e] z.

Line 4.

1. Sing f[ɔ]r, not f[ə]r.
2. Mercy is one of many words we sing with too much "r." When r is in the middle of a word before a consonant, omit it entirely. Sing m[ɜ]-c[ɪ].
3. Sing p[a e] thus, not p[ɑ]ths.
4. [ʌ]f is desirable over [ə]f because it is sung on a quarter note. Sing [ə]f only on short notes.
5. Sing [ɪ]ce on the release. Be sure it is heard or the word sounds gr[ɛ]c rather than gr[eɪ]c.

Consonants

There are two kinds of consonants, voiced and unvoiced (pitched and unpitched). Sing an initial voiced consonant on the same pitch as the vowel it precedes. Sing a final voiced consonant on the same pitch as the vowel it follows. Sing an unaccented [ə] (uh) at the end of words ending in b, d, and g (buh, duh, and guh), but not on the other voiced consonants. Unvoiced consonants have no definite pitch. They are articulated by the breath blowing through the openings made by the lips, tongue, teeth and palate.

How To Teach Unvoiced and Voiced Articulation

Place the following list on a blackboard:

articulation	*unvoiced*	*voiced*
lips forward	rope	ro<u>b</u>e sung rob<u>uh</u> [ə]
lips back	<u>wh</u>ich (blow the <u>h</u> through the lips	wi<u>t</u>ch (sung (<u>oo</u>itch)
bottom lip— top teeth	lea<u>f</u>	leave (sustain the <u>v</u>; no <u>uh</u> ending)
tongue against gum ridge	ro<u>t</u>e	ro<u>d</u>e (sung ro<u>d</u>uh [ə])
tongue—teeth	wid<u>th</u>	wi<u>th</u> (no <u>uh</u> ending)
tongue and hard palate	sear<u>ch</u>	sur<u>ge</u> (no <u>uh</u> ending)
tongue and hard palate	ice (<u>s</u> sound)	eyes (<u>z</u> sound—no <u>uh</u> ending)
tongue and hard palate	ocean (<u>sh</u> sound)	vi<u>si</u>on (sing the con- sonant with the second syllable)
tongue and soft palate	bro<u>k</u>e	bro<u>q</u>ue (sung bro<u>g</u>uh)

Ask the chorus to sing ro<u>p</u>e and ro<u>buh</u> and note that the <u>p</u> and <u>b</u>uh are articulated with the lips. The <u>p</u> is exploded; the <u>b</u> is resonated. The chorus must learn the importance of voiced articulation to intelligent word sense; voiced consonants sung without resonance change word meanings drastically; God becomes got, cold changes to colt, etc.

Rules for Consonants

1. The lip consonants are <u>p</u> and <u>b</u>, <u>f</u> and <u>v</u>, <u>w</u> and <u>wh</u>, and <u>m</u>. Sound the <u>p</u>, <u>f</u>, and <u>w</u> by blowing a puff of breath through the

[ə]

lips at the moment of articulation. Sing the b (buh), w (oo) and m on the same pitch as the vowel which precedes or follows the consonant. Sustain the v, w, and m long enough to be heard by the audience. Never add the uh sound to them; sing love, not lovuh; them, not themuh.

2. The tongue and teeth consonants are th (as in thin) and th (as in the). Articulate the voiceless th with the lips touching the bottom of the top teeth. Do not protrude the tongue too far. Blow breath the instant of articulation. Form the voiced th the same way, but add the pitch of the preceding or following vowel to the sound. Do not add an uh ending; sing with, not withuh.

3. The gum-ridge consonants are t, d, b, and n. The tip of the tongue touches the upper gum. Do not form the t, d or n with the teeth closed. Sustain l and n long enough to be heard. Never add the uh ending. Once the singer knows how to form the consonant correctly, he should articulate by aural image—not thinking consciously about the articulators.

4. The hard-palate consonants are s and z, sh and s (as in usual), ch and soft g (j and y as in yeast).

S and z, sh and s (as in usual), ch and soft g (j) are sibilants, that is, hissing and buzzing sounds. Minimize unvoiced s, sh and ch by giving careful attention to attacks and releases. Release the tongue downward the instant the sound is made to avoid the hissss. Singing sibilants with the teeth closed causes too much of the hissing sound.

Z sounds are formed exactly like the s, but resonated. Substitution of s for z produces such words as rice for rize, rose for the beautiful roze, real lice for realize. One s sound penetrates through the whole chorus. Those who cannot resonate the sound have to omit the zz's completely.

Y is a semivowel at the beginning of words such as you or yield, a vowel [I] in words such as myth, and the diphthong [ɑI] in the words by and rye, etc. Avoid singing atchour for at your. Lightly toss the y precisely on the beat.

5. The soft palate consonants are k, g, ng. To form these consonants, place the back of the tongue against or close to the soft palate. Explode the k. Sing hard g with the unaccented [ə] (uh) on the same pitch as the vowel immediately before or after it; otherwise, God sounds cod, log sounds lock. Ng is a nasal. The mouth remains open, the soft palate and tongue touch, the vibrating air column goes into the nasal passage. Do not add uh to the sound. Sing sing, not singuh.

6. Rules for the consonant r. The r can be rolled, flipped or Americanized. Form the American r by turning the tongue upward toward the roof of the mouth without touching it. We do not use the rolled or flipped r in American English. However, they are useful tools. Some teachers change the r sound to [ə]. I prefer to hear some r sound.

7. How to teach students to roll and flip r's: Begin with the sound hudd[ə]r. Sing the sound with a relaxed tongue. Say the word over and over rapidly until d[ə]r begins to flip. Relax the tongue—let it go. Think of blowing the [ə]r into the flip or roll. Use your imagination. Imagine the rolled r silently; sing it aloud.

8. The aspirate h consonant: Articulate the aspirate h through the opening of the next vowel. For example, in singing, the muscles are set for the vowel oh; the aspirate is blown through the oh opening, and the vowel is sung. Without enough h, hand sounds and, harm sounds arm, and hit sounds it.

9. Other uses for "h." Some directors interpolate h between notes in running (florid) passages. (See Figure 7-4.)

Figure 7-4

Pro-pter ma-gnum glo - $h_oh_oh_o$- $h_oh_oh_oh_oh_oh_oh_oh$ -h_o- ri- am

I do not recommend the interpolated h in this way for three reasons: First, too much aspirate makes the tone breathy; second, throat muscles are used to articulate the h that should not be used; third, a passage sung this way often sounds like sung laughter.

Let the singing in the imagination take care of the articulation. Singers can sing aloud as fast as they can sing in their imaginations. The h merely discourages a singer from trusting his imagination to guide his voice. If you desire a marcato on running passages, imagine a light toss on each note. This will give the same effect as a light h, but without the breathiness that accompanies the h. Those who use the h effectively have their choristers think it rather than actually articulate it.

10. Sometimes nasals (n, m, and ng) end words in climaxes and at other key places. They need emphasis. The climax of *O Rejoice Ye Christians Loudly* by Bach ends: "For the Son of Grace is Shining." The ing needs to be both accented and clipped to be interpretatively effective. Imagine a strong accent on the ng and release immediately. The sound is heard and the emotion felt. Do not sing shininguh.

The n in some amens can be sustained; for example, the final n in the sevenfold amen. The final amen in Handel's "Hallelu-jah" from *Judas Maccabaeus* needs the accented clipped release. (See Figure 7-5.) Accent the final n and clip it off. By aural

Figure 7-5

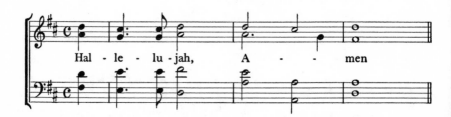

image, sing the n as loudly as the preceding (eh) vowel. *Never* add (uh) to the word. Sing amennnn, never amenuh.

11. To maintain word sense, certain rules of word separation must be observed. Words are connected in legato passages except when a connection changes the meaning of a key word; (us in) sounds (a sin) when the s is sung on the beat and not separated from the word in.

> (Flesh he) sounds (fleshshe) or (fleshy)
> (jealous eyes) sounds (jealous sighs)
> (its not) sounds (it's snot)

There are two ways to avoid incorrect word connections:

1. Imagine a light aspirate h between a word ending with a consonant and one beginning with a vowel. The h is imagined more than sung.

2. Imagine a light toss on the initial vowel or consonant of the second word. This forces singers to articulate the preceding consonant a split second before the beat. The light toss eliminates many diction problems, including incorrect word separations. Sing the phrase in Figure 7-6. Articulate the final consonants on the beat as indicated (the wrong way).

Figure 7-6

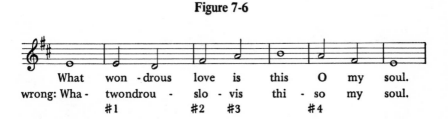

Solutions (the correct way):

1. Sing a soft t; lightly toss the oo on the beat. Do not sing the t on the beat.

2. Lightly toss the l–sing the vowel on the beat.

3. Sing the <u>v</u> on the same pitch as the preceding vowel and/or interpolate a light <u>h</u>.

4. Mentally toss <u>o</u> on the beat or think the interpolated <u>h</u> before <u>o</u>.

Sing the song with these rules and notice how the natural inflections of the words result from applying them.

I analyzed the consonants in Figure 7-7 to illustrate some problems and solutions.

Soprano part of <u>My Heart Is Offered Still to You</u>

Di Lassus

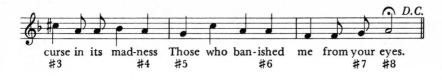

curse in its mad-ness Those who ban-ished me from your eyes.
#3   #4   #5   #6   #7   #8

Figure 7-7

Analysis of Figure 7-7

Line 1.

#1. Words containing r followed by a consonant are sung with too much r sound. Omit the r but don't settle for h[ɑ]t (hot). Imagine [ə] with t (h[ɑ]-[ə]t). Have your chorus practice singing *hot* followed by *heart* for a clear definition of these two words.

#2. Sing the t against the roof of the mouth and lightly toss the word (is) to avoid tis.

#3. Omit the r sound.

#4. Toss the y to avoid the inevitable slur.

#5. Toss of to avoid wof.

#6. One d sung on pitch c².

#7. Lightly toss the ing to avoid misplacing the accent; the r will sound before the beat. Otherwise, the words sound spare-ring. Sing ng, not n.

Line 2.

#1. Omit the first t.

#2. Sound the n's in constancy on the preceding pitches.

#3. Toss the tr to avoid an intermittent vowel tuhrue.

#4. Omit the r; toss the w to avoid a slur.

#5. Omit the first r. Lightly toss the second one.

#6. Sing *row* on the first part of the diphthong. Articulate the second sound after the pitch a¹ is sung.

#7. & 8. These are the same as #6 & 8 in line 1.

Line 3.

#1. Sustain m's for smooth line.

#2. Sound the aspirate h through lips formed for [ɯ] (ooh).

#3. Toss k sound to avoid scould smile. The toss separates the s from the c.

#4. Sing l on pitch e¹ ; toss in.

#5. Do not sing gladuhness. Implode the d.

#6. Implode the d.

#7. Omit the r. Sing the m on the preceding pitch f¹ .

#8. Sing ng, not n.

#9. Sing z, not s.

#10. Sing z, not s.

Line 4.

#1. Articulate the n on pitch b¹ and the l on pitch d² .

#2. Explode a strong k for emotional accent.

#3. Toss in, or interpolate a light h to avoid a misplaced accent.

#4. Implode the d to avoid maduhness.

#5. Sing z, not s—articulate the aspirate h on who.

#6. Avoid too much sibilant sound.

#7. Toss *eyes* to avoid *your rize*, or interpolate h (your heyes).

#8. Sing z, not s.

Emotional Diction

Text presentations embrace more than mere mechanics. Texts have an inborn rhythm and tempo; multi-syllabic words have strong and weak inflections; each line of poetry and prose expresses a particular emotion and/or idea; key words need consonant and dynamic emphasis, while auxiliary words are unaccented. To teach correct word inflections, have everyone speak the text in rhythm on a single pitch. (See Figure 7-8.)

Figure 7-8

Study the following text for rhythm, tempo, word inflection, sentence meaning, and key words. Begin by reciting aloud. Note the poetic scansion.

      stressed inflection   unstressed inflection

Line 1. April is in my mistress' face,

Line 2. and July in her eyes hath place

Line 3. within her bo - som is September

Line 4. But in her heart a cold December.

Lines 1, 2 and 3 seemingly describe the perfect girl. Line 4 puts a whole new meaning on the poem.

Suggestions for an Emotional Text Interpretation

Line 1. Emphasize the l̲, n̲, and two m̲'s for a smooth and intense line. The beauty and awe of spring permeates the phrase. To obtain intensity, recite the line with little or no inflection.

Line 2. July reaffirms with less intensity her loveliness. Because it is less intense, inflect more, emphasizing the key words *July*, *eyes*, *place*. Mentally toss *eyes* or interpolate an h̲ to avoid singing her rize. (The old English pronunciation for July is Ju'l[I].)

Line 3. Nature has reached its mature beauty. The girl is physically beautiful in every respect. Speak the line smoothly, with more intensity, at a slower tempo. Say the m in boso<u>m</u> before you articulate <u>is</u>; bosom <u>is</u>, not boso-miz.

Line 4. This phrase reaches the emotional peak of the poem. Stress the key words, <u>but, heart, cold</u> and de<u>cem</u>ber. Strongly articulate the underlined consonants—strong <u>h</u> aspirate in heart, exploded <u>k</u>, linger on the <u>l</u> before saying a single strong <u>d</u> for both words.

How To Get an Emotional Response from Your Choristers

1. Discuss the meaning of the text.
2. Recite the text at different tempos, at various dynamic and pitch levels.
3. Determine the key words. Practice emphasizing the key words by both inflection and consonant stress.
4. Guide and cajole. Demonstrate! Pull the meaning out of your singer's.
5. Give mechanical directions only after the choir understands the emotional impact of a text, and then only as an expedient.

Let us compare the inherent mood, tempo, dynamic level, and degree of inflection of the two fold songs printed in Figures 7-9a and 7-9b. (Both can be found in choral arrangements.) See Figures 7-9a and 7-9b.

Johnny Has Gone for a Soldier

American Folk Song

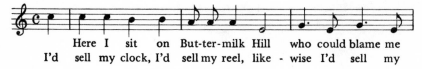

Here I sit on But-ter-milk Hill who could blame me
I'd sell my clock, I'd sell my reel, like - wise I'd sell my

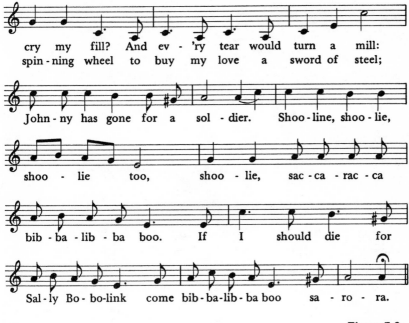

cry my fill? And ev - 'ry tear would turn a mill:
spin - ning wheel to buy my love a sword of steel;

John - ny has gone for a sol - dier. Shoo - line, shoo - lie,

shoo - lie too, shoo - lie, sac - ca - rac - ca

bib - ba - lib - ba boo. If I should die for

Sal - ly Bo - bo-link come bib - ba - lib - ba boo sa - ro - ra.

Figure 7-9a

Early One Morning

Ear -ly one morn -ing, just as the sun was ris - ing,
Re - mem- ber the vows that you made to your Mar - y,
Oh, gay is the gar - land, and fresh are the ros - es
Thus sang the poor maid - en, her sor - row be - wail - ing,

I heard a maid sing in the val - ley be - low.
Re - mem - ber the bow'r where you vowed to be true.
I've culled from the gar - den to bind on thy brow.
Thus sang the poor maid in the val - ley be - low.

Oh! don't de - ceive me, Oh! nev - er leave me,

Figure 7-9b

Text Analysis:

Johnny Has Gone for a Soldier	*Early One Morning*
Mood:	*Mood:*
intense, heartrending. In the chorus are thoughts too difficult to express with words. Very personal.	impersonal—the story is about someone else. Fun-poking, but not without an element of pathos.
Tempo:	*Tempo:*
Slow.	Moderate. Too fast a tempo destroys all feeling for the girl's dilemma.
Dynamic Level:	*Dynamic Level:*
Generally soft on first verse and chorus. Somewhat louder on second verse because it's an action verse. Verse 1 tells how you feel; verse 2 tells what you would do about it.	Verse 1: medium. Verse 2: softer. Verse 3: louder. Verse 4: soft. The chorus follows the dynamics of each verse.
Degree of Inflection:	*Degree of Inflection:*
Verse 1, hardly any inflection; verse 2, much inflection; chorus, little inflection.	Natural inflections on verse 1, 2 and 3. Less inflection on verse 4.

The style of both songs in Figures 7-9a and 7-9b grows out of text considerations. To create the emotional intensity in verse 1 of *"Johnny"*, elongate the l, m, n, ng consonants. A light toss on initial consonants and vowels in *Early One Morning* keeps it in a lighter style. Verse 4 can be smoother, more intense. By so doing the interpreter shows there is some compassion in his heart for the young girl's feelings.

Whispering—An Auxiliary Technique

Whispering texts in rhythm helps defeat consonant lethargy. Since there is no pitch involved, mental concentration can be on consonant articulation exclusively.

Rules:

1. Use the technique when consonants are not "clicking" with precision on fast tempos.
2. Whisper "to the back of the auditorium."
3. Do not overuse. Too much whispering causes dry throats and tires the vocal mechanism.
4. Use whispering as an auxiliary to aural image—not as a substitute.

Latin Pronunciation

Thus far I have limited my discussion to "American" English. Although more high school choruses sing foreign languages today, the bulk of their singing is still in English. No book of this scope can go into all the intricacies of every language. I have tried to touch upon only the most important problems of our own language.

Fine choral music with Latin texts is plentiful and often within the technical scope of high schoolers. Liturgical (church) Latin pronunciation has no diphthongs; the vowels are pure and the r's are always flipped. Many colloquial language habits can be cured by singing in Latin, with its pure vowels.

A Latin Pronunciation Chart

a–[ɑ] (ah) as in father.

e– sound like [e] as in chaos. Do not diphthongize. It is better
to sing [ɛ] (eh) than [eɪ].

ae and oe–pronounced like e vowel (see above).

i–[j] as in see–in sounds een, not [ɪ]n.

o–sound [o] as in obey. Do not diphthongize. It is better to
sing [ɔ] than [ou] or [ou].

u–sounds [ʊ] (ōōh) as in prune.

au–sounds [ɑ] [ʊ] (ahōōh).

c–before i, e, ae, and oe, sound ch. Before all other vowels, k.

ch–sounds k.

g–soft before e, i, ae, and oe.

gn–sounds [ny] –magnum sounds manyum.

h–silent except in mihi and mihil.

j–sounds like y (as in you).

r–is always flipped or rolled.

t–is soft (ts) when preceded by a vowel and when followed by
the vowels e, i, ae, oe.

th–sounds t as in Thomas.

x–sounds gs as in eggs or as x.

sc–sounds sh before e, i, ae and oe.

y–sounds [i] (ee)

Examples:

IPA [ɛ] [i] [ɛ] [ɑ] [ɑ] [o]   [i]   [i]   [u]

Et in   ter ra   pax ho mi – ni – bus.

eht een teh-rrrah pahx how – mee – nee – boohs.

[ɛ]   [u]   [ɑ] [e] [e]   [o] [ɑ]   [o]   [i]

Ex – ul – ta – te De – o   ad – to – ri

ehgs – ooh – tah – teh deh – aw   ahd – taw – ree

[o] [o]

no-stro

naw-straw

[i] [u] [ɑ] [ɑ] [i] [ɛ] [i] [ɑ]

In   tu -a   pa- ti-   en-   ti - a

een tooh-ah   pah-tsee- ehn -tsee -ah

[e] [ɑ] [i]   [ɑ] [i]   [ɑ] [ɑ] [o]

De   cas- ti   ta - tis   tha -la -mo

Deh cah-stee   tah-tsees   tah -lah -maw

[ɛ] *eh* and [ɔ] *aw* are often substituted for the sounds [e]
and [o] .

Release of Articulation Muscles

The articulation muscles we can control consciously are the
mandible (jaw), tongue, lips, facial muscles, and the soft palate.
All muscles respond neurologically. However, some muscles
habitually tense because of incorrect training and/or wrong
concepts. William Finn writes: "Singing is guided solely by
mental control, the actual sound being generated by reflex
processes."[2] Articulators reflex according to what messages we
send. The articulation muscles release when we learn to sing the
right sound in the imagination and sing aloud simultaneously.

Articulation Misconceptions

I draw attention to physical problems only when students
persist in singing physically. Their persistence is usually due to
misconceptions about articulation.

Misconception: the jaw should fall open on every vowel.

Fact: The position that results from dropping the jaw is the

---

2. William Finn, *The Art of the Choral Conductor*, Vol. I (Boston: C. C. Birchard
and Co., 1939), p. 233.

worst position—either the jaw should be more closed or more open. Students who guide their voices by their imaginations sing with a variety of jaw positions depending on how high and low, how loud and soft, the speed of the song, and the particular sounds they are articulating. This is how it should be.

Misconception: the tongue lays flat in the mouth on the vowel *ah* and has a groove in it.

Fact: Zangwill discovered in his experiments that this is a false assumption. He writes: "It is shown that not all speech sounds entail characteristic lip positions and that there is in general less rigidity in vocal postures than is commonly supposed. For instance, the position of the tongue formerly deemed essential to pronunciation of particular speech sounds in fact shows considerable variability."[3] The tongue moves a great deal to help form vowels and consonants. On *ah* vowels, a grooved tongue can improve the vowel only *if* the groove is natural to the singer.

Misconception: lips and cheeks (facial muscles) are moved as little as possible to obtain relaxation.

Fact: Movement does not mean tension. These muscles move when properly innervated. If they are not allowed to move, they cannot do their share of the work in clear articulation. Less efficient muscles have to make up for them, and tension in the throat results.

Misconception: the soft palate must be consciously raised against the pharynx wall. Some singers think it helps to sing in the yawn.

Fact: The soft palate will raise or lower in response to correct messages sent by singing in the imagination. Mechanical methods tense the muscles and cause a hard tone quality because too many overtones remain in the tone.

---

3. L. Zangwill, "Neurophysiology," *Handbook of Physiology*, Vol III (Washington: American Physiology Society, 1960), p. 1715.

The Diagastric Muscles

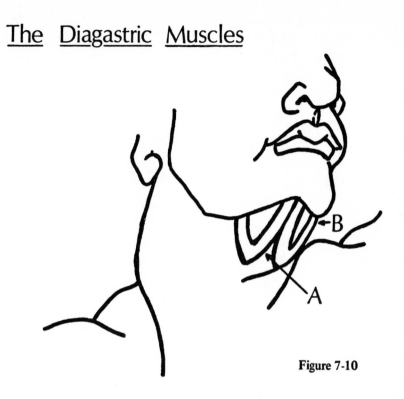

Figure 7-10

Place your thumb at *A* and your forefinger at *B*. Swallow. These are your diagastric muscles. These muscles are used in swallowing and should be released when we speak or sing. If they are pushed down and are tight when we speak and sing, the resultant sounds are incorrect. Check a student's progress by touching these spots to feel how tight or free the muscles are. Do not push upward against the muscles. Use them as a progress guide. When your students' speech is free and imitated exactly when they sing, these muscles automatically release. When the diagastric muscles are tense, it is because the student does not allow his imagined sounds to determine the muscular action of the articulation muscles. He is still trying to make sounds physically. Sing in the imagination and release without hesitation or critical judgment.

CHAPTER 8

Classifying Voices for the High School Chorus

Testing voices and classifying them as sopranos, altos, tenors, basses, and their subdivisions is an important part of our role as choral directors. Vocal problems result when we incorrectly classify a singer and permit him to remain in a wrong classification for any length of time. We have two major and sometimes conflicting duties to perform when we select our choruses each year: First, we must determine which section is best for each singer's vocal health and development, and second, we must select from the singers who apply a group of singers who have a potential to become a balanced and good-sounding chorus.

In order to get a better choral balance than nature provides for us, we sometimes place singers into sections in which they do not belong; that is, baritones in the tenor section and/or second bass section, and sopranos in the alto section. This is a dangerous practice, but one that is often expedient if we are to have balanced high school choruses. I believe we need to sacrifice our choral program for the individual singer and do our best to place each singer into the classification which best suits his natural endowment. This chapter attempts to show how we can have good choral ensembles and still classify voices correctly.

Types of Voices

Voices divide into six main categories: bass, baritone, tenor, alto, mezzo-soprano and soprano. These can be divided into subtypes: dramatic, spinto, lyric and coloratura. The dramatic and spinto subtypes seldom reveal themselves in young voices. Vennard recommends that all young voices, no matter what main category they belong to, should be classified lyric. He writes: "It is foolhardy and a little ridiculous for a young singer to classify himself as 'Dramatic'."[1]

Choral groups normally divide into first and second sopranos, first and second altos, first and second tenors, baritones, and basses. Lighter voices sing the first parts (upper notes) and the heavier voices sing the second parts. (See Figure 8-1.)

In mature choruses, the coloratura and lyric sopranos sing first parts while the spinto and dramatic sopranos sing second parts. Dramatic and spinto voices do not exist in high school choruses. Color differentiations in a teen-age chorus are best achieved by placing heavier voices on second parts and lighter voices on first parts.

True altos are rare in high school choruses. These parts often are assigned to girls who have the vocal physiology of a soprano who has not discovered her upper timbres. These girls usually speak far below their optimum pitch level and have poor timbres, but they can read music. The practice of classifying potential sopranos as altos because they read music should be avoided. When you have a scarcity of true altos, supplement the section with some of your good reading sopranos *but* have the sopranos take turns so that none sing the alto tessitura for more

---

1. Vennard, *Singing: The Mechanism and the Technic*, p. 79.

Figure 8-1

CHORAL CLASSIFICATIONS	PROFESSIONAL CLASSIFICATIONS
soprano 1 - light	coloratura soprano lyric soprano
soprano 11 - heavy	lyric spinto soprano dramatic soprano
alto 1 - light	mezzo-soprano mezzo-contralto
alto 11 - heavy	contralto counter-tenor
tenor 1 - light	lyric tenor lyric spinto tenor
tenor 11 - heavy	dramatic tenor lyric baritone
bass 1 - Baritones	lyric baritone baritone
bass 11 - basses	bass baritone bass

than one or two numbers. Another way to help avoid vocal suicide for a young alto section is to have the section sing the soprano part as soon as their alto notes are secure. (If your readers are in the alto section, they will be the first to learn their pitches.)

Tenor parts are often assigned to high baritones who do not have the stamina to maintain the tenor tessitura. It is sometimes difficult in young voices to distinguish between a true baritone and a tenor who has not yet discovered his upper timbres.

Generally, low basses are rare among young singers. Baritones need protection from singing in a bass tessitura all the time. Sociological factors seem to influence maturation rate. Vocal maturity exists in city schools and within ethnic groups more than in suburban and rural areas.

Although distinctions between some teen-age voices are difficult to discern, we can make use of several tools in our attempts to do so. It is important to make every effort possible to classify voices correctly. Singers who are incorrectly classified emphasize a set of laryngeal muscles that are detrimental to their instruments. Further, they produce false vocal qualities which are even more damaging than wrong tessitura. Baritones who sing in a low bass tessitura darken their natural sound in an attempt to sound like low basses; tenors in a baritone section likewise; sopranos singing alto parts overemphasize chest timbre. Anyone singing in a tessitura unsuitable to his natural physiology is forced to sing with mixed timbres and will end up unable to develop his voice to its fullest potential.

How To Classify Voices

Unfortunately there is no sure-fire scientific way to classify voices. Anatomical measurements of the larynx and classification of voices by neural measurements have been expounded, but these methods are neither practical nor generally accepted as valid. We are forced to use our ears as the final authority. I recommend a classification system based on a study of each singer's range, tessitura, and timbre, his optimum pitch for speaking, and the notes on which he changes from one timbre to another (transition notes). All of the findings of each individual test are recorded on an audition form. (See Figure 8-2.)

Figure 8-2

Voice Classification Audition Form

Name _____

Address _____City_____State_____

Telephone_____Voice part usually sung_____

Range	Tessitura	Vocal quality
		Soprano_____
		Alto _____
		Tenor _____
		Bass_____

Optimum speaking pitch	Quality	Transition notes
	Sop._____	
	Alto._____	
	Tenor_____	
	Bass_____	

Voice part assigned_____

Range

Figure 8-3 shows the range of each voice classification. The whole notes encompass the more common ranges; the black notes show extreme ranges. Ranges are narrower for teen-age voices, and such categories as contralto I and II are non-existent. Since no two voices are identical, the above ranges serve only as guidelines. Beginning choristers seldom know the full extent of their ranges and because a natural or trained bass can sing higher than a mediocre baritone, and good baritones can sing higher than tenors who have not discovered their upper timbres, etc., range is the least reliable consideration in classifying teen-age voices. Nevertheless, it serves as one of the criteria on which we base our classification of voices.

Step 1 to classifying voices: check the range (both ascending and descending) and place it on the singer's classification audition form (Figure 8-2:)

Range Classification Chart

Figure 8-3

Tessitura

A scientific method for determining a singer's tessitura apparently does not exist. The following empirical approach is time consuming, but at present the only approach available.

While the student sings a five-tone ascending and descending scale (do re mi fa so fa mi re do), determine by your ear which notes sound best and seem most free. Check your findings against the notes the student felt were the easiest to produce. Check your findings against the tessitura chart in Figure 8-4.

Tessitura Classification Chart

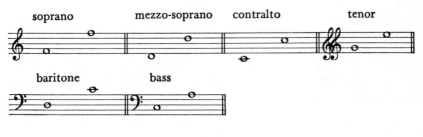

Figure 8-4

Step 2 to classifying voices: check the notes on each singer's range that are easiest to produce (his diagnosis) and which sound best (your diagnosis). Test until you and the student agree on the same pitches. Place these pitches on the singer's audition form.

Timbre

Most voice teachers consider the singer's quality the most important element in voice classification. However, we know that the vocal mechanism is capable of producing qualities that are artificial (and therefore injurious) to the voice. Because timbre is initiated in the cortex, a student can produce any timbre he can imagine (limited only by his anatomical structure). Therefore, a voice cannot be classified on the basis of timbre until a singer's true vocal quality reveals itself.

Speaking on higher pitch levels and imitating the speech

when singing reveals a singer's natural quality in contrast to his habitual quality.

Step 3 to classifying voices: determine the quality of the singer as **you** test him for range and tessitura. Then have him speak on several pitch levels and transfer the speech to singing. Check the resultant quality against what he sounds like habitually, and place your appraisal on the audition form.

Optimum Pitch

The exercise for establishing optimum pitch level for speaking (see Chapter One) helps us establish both the tessitura and the vocal quality of the singer. Have the singer speak a short phrase, such as, "how are you today ⁔," on pitches from a_ to g² at full volume. (See Figure 8-5.) Notice the pitches that sound full, free, and easiest to produce. These should represent an area of about five steps. Check this against the test you gave for tessitura. The tessitura and optimum speech area should be the same. Note the quality and check this against your earlier appraisal made of the student's singing voice.

Step 4 to classifying voices: determine tessitura and quality through the test for optimum pitch for speaking. Record your findings on the audition form.

Pitch names used throughout this book follow the system shown below.

C - B   c   -   b   c1 - b1 c2 - b2 c3

Figure 8-5

Transition Notes

Another method of classifying voices that is particularly valid for trained or natural singers is referred to as the transition note method. The singer ascends and descends a five note scale (do re mi fa so fa mi re do) and/or descends a five note scale (so fa mi re do). The auditioner determines the note on which the singer changes from one timbre (register) to the other. Those who change from middle timbre to upper timbre on the note $\underline{f}^{\#2}$ are classified as sopranos (tenors, an octave lower), those who change from middle timbre to upper timbre on $\underline{e}^{b2}$ are mezzo-sopranos (baritones, an octave lower), and those who change from middle to upper timbre on $\underline{d}^2$ are contraltos (basses, an octave lower).

The auditioner then checks the transition note on which the singer changes from middle timbre to chest timbre. Sopranos and tenors change on $\underline{f}^1$, mezzo-sopranos and baritones change on $\underline{e}^{b1}$ or $\underline{d}^1$.

Transition notes are more easily discerned when your students speak than when they sing. Check the speech timbre changes you heard during the optimum pitch test (above) against the changes you hear when the student sings.

The student must be singing full voice throughout his range before the transition points have validity. Any sudden loss or gain in intensity (volume) indicates he should have changed timbres but didn't. Young voice students usually cannot maintain an equal volume throughout their range. Consequently, it becomes difficult to tell where young singers' natural transition notes are. After working through the aural image techniques in the foregoing chapters, these transition notes begin to show themselves. Nevertheless, they are worth noting even in the first stages of training.

Step 5 to classifying voices: listen to the singer and record on his audition form the pitches on which he changes from one timbre to another when the singer maintains full volume throughout his range.

Summary:

There are five steps in classifying voices:

Step 1—Range
Step 2—Tessitura
Step 3—Timbre
Step 4—Optimum pitch for speaking
Step 5—Transition notes

These five steps checked against one another give the auditioner a good picture of each singer's voice classification. We must remember, however, that physiological changes are constantly taking place in teen-age voices and frequent re-testing is necessary. Each high school director should establish in his schedule time to hear all of his choristers at least three times a year: in the fall before the chorus rehearsals begin, and during exam weeks at the end of each semester. Hear those students who are new or who were particularly difficult to classify at mid-term of the first semester as well. As a student learns to implement aural image techniques, all of the classification considerations become more clearly defined. By the end of a year's training in aural image technique, each student's true vocal endowment becomes apparent.

It is important to keep our goals before us. In the fall we should select music for our chorus that does not tax our students' range and tessitura. This is especially true if we have had to classify voices before their natural quality has been exposed.

CHAPTER 9

Selecting Music for the High School Chorus

LUCHSINGER WRITES: "MOST experienced investigators recommend that systematic singing instruction should not be
started before the age of 17 in girls or before 18 or 19 in boys
living in the Temperate Zone."[1] Some authorities from foreign
countries believe teen-age boys should stop singing altogether
during the period of voice change. The reasons generally given
include:

1. Drastic physiological changes take place during early puber-
ty. Girls' vocal folds grow about 2 to 4 mm. longer, while boys'
vocal folds grow about 1 cm. longer.
2. Muscles within the larynx grow at varying rates, making
coordination difficult. They are in a constant state of flux.
3. A different type of innervation is required during the growth
of the larynges.

Music educators know the physiological facts concerning the
changes that take place during teen-age years. Most of us know

---

1. Richard Luchsinger and Godfrey Arnold, *Voice–Speech Language*, 1965, p. 133.

that young people can and do sing during adolescence and believe our job, as educators, is to guide their vocal development through these crucial years. Our success as high school vocal teachers depends on several factors: (1) a knowledge that aural image, not conscious muscular effort, hold the key to good singing; (2) our ability to implement this knowledge in a methodical and effective way; (3) our ability to classify voices correctly; (4) a realization that music for high school choruses is selected according to the singers' physiological maturation and training; (5) cognizance that physiological factors determine range, tessitura and dynamic limitations; (6) a recognition that many boys' voices are still changing during high school and need special range considerations.

Teen-agers acquire high proficiency levels on musical instruments other than the voice. They master sight-reading, play in tune, obtain efficient technique, and perform with phrase sense. Often their minds are developed to cope with musical problems before their voices are.

Conductors damage voices when they select music that pushes voices beyond their physical maturation. Teen-age vocal muscles develop slowly over a long period of time. The director must choose music comparable to the innate talent and musical training of his choristers without damaging their immature instruments, and he must stay within vocal limitations and still select music of aesthetic and social value.

Technical Considerations in Music Selection

Technical considerations include range, tessitura and dynamic intensity. These considerations outweigh all others by far. Music that looks easy melodically and rhythmically proves difficult when it oversteps the youngsters' ranges and tessituras.

Most voice teachers agree that these are the main considerations in music selection for young singers. Some private and college voice teachers hesitate to allow their students to participate in choral groups because of the demands the music makes on voices. It is up to us to avoid this kind of reaction to our choral programs by giving careful attention to the range, tessitura and dynamic demands of the music we choose for our choruses.

Range

Range defines (1) the extreme notes a singer can sing musically, and (2) the extreme notes of a vocal line in a composition. "Correct" ranges put forth by authors vary greatly. The ranges in Figure 9-1 resulted from a study of ranges recommended by vocal authorities placed in light of my own experiences. These notes show the safe ranges of a vocal composition for high school voices. (See Figure 9-1.)

Music selection range chart

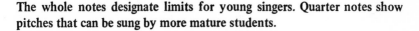

The whole notes designate limits for young singers. Quarter notes show pitches that can be sung by more mature students.

Figure 9-1

Range considerations in music selection are:

1. Select music for the less mature students. Freshmen and sophomores have smaller ranges than juniors and seniors.
2. Keep ranges narrow in the beginning of each school year. Broaden them as the year progresses, voices mature, and aural image technique develops.
3. Have the more mature and experienced singers sing the extreme notes. Compose more comfortable notes for the others.

4. Interchange low alto and high tenor notes. Many works fit the given range limitations when we redistribute voice parts.

Tessitura

The Tessitura of the Voice:

Tessitura is the singer's comfortable range. Victor Alexander Fields defines it as: "That part of the vocal range that can be sung with ease for some time."[2]

Authorities agree that beginning voice students should limit most of their singing within their tessituras; that is, somewhere in the middle of their ranges. Where this middle area falls varies from one authority to another. All agree that each individual has a tessitura unique to himself.

Tessitura of a Composition:

Fields describes the tessitura of a composition as: "That part of the melody or voice part of a musical composition in which most of its tones lie."[3] Many authors acknowledge tessitura of a composition as an important factor in music selection but none, to my knowledge, includes a satisfactory means of determining it.

How To Determine the Tessitura of a Composition

Practical experience teaches directors which compositions work or fail in their choral groups. As I analyzed many compositions that worked and failed for my high school choirs, a pattern of tessitura limitations began to take shape. Without exception the compositions that "sounded" had limited tessitura, and vice versa. How could I predetermine the success of a

---

2. Victor Alexander Fields, *Training the Singing Voice* (New York: Kings Crown Press, 1947), p. 50.

3. *Loc. cit.*

composition on the basis of tessitura? First, I studied compositions that were successful. From these I developed a set of tessituras that works for high school voices. (See Figure 9-2.) Then I tried to discover an infallible way to determine what the

Music Selection Tessitura Chart

Figure 9-2

tessitura of each composition was. By careful scrutiny of the score I was able to calculate where most of the beats lay. Immediately my choices of compositions improved. Later I devised a more dependable method. It took longer but the results were worth the extra time. Here are the simple steps:

Step 1. First make a chart like the one in Figure 9-3 and mimeograph several copies of it. (See Figure 9-3.)

Step 2. Count the number of beats of each note in each voice part and write the totals on the chart.

Step 3. Total the number of beats of each voice part.

Step 4. Determine that no more than 10 percent to 12 percent of the beats lie outside of the tessitura.

Step 5. Draw lines to show on the chart exactly what the tessitura of each voice part is.

Step 6. Compare these findings with the tessitura chart I established for high school voices (Figure 9-2).

Figure 9-3

Composition ___Ave Verum___   Composer ___Mozart___

Publisher ___Generally available___

Number of beats

soprano		alto		tenor		bass	
a2	-	e2	-	a1	-	e1	-
g2	-	d2	-	g1	-	d1	-
f2	-	c2	-	f1	-	c1	-
e2	-1	b1	-	e1	-3	b	-8
d2	-17	a1	-5	d1	-18	a	-23
c2	-4	g1	-8	c1	-37	g	-15
b1	-7.5	f1	-20	b	-24	f	-13
a1	-37.5	e1	-60	a	-44	e	-9
g1	-37	d1	-31	g	-8	d	-25
f1	-20	c1	-17	·f	-4	c	-14
e1	-20	b	-1	e	-2	b	-7
d1	-5	a	-	d	-9	a	-22
c1	-	g	-	c	-	g	-1
	149		142		140		137

totals:

Analysis:

The bulk of the beats lie as follows: soprano, $\underline{e}^1 - \underline{d}^2$; alto, $\underline{c}^1 - \underline{f}^1$; tenor, $\underline{a} - \underline{d}^1$; bass, $\underline{A} - \underline{a}$. The soprano, alto, and tenor tessitura are excellent. The bass is one-half step low. The maturity of the bass section should determine when they could sing this selection, since they sing several $\underline{A}$'s. Further examination of the bass part reveals several places where the lighter basses can sing the A̲'s an octave higher and others where they can sing E a fifth higher; for example, the cadence after the first climax. (See Figure 9-4.)

*edited note for baritones

Figure 9-4

Sixteen beats can be altered this way. Your high school baritones can sing A̲'s, but a limitation of them is recommended. Let us examine some other compositions by the above tessitura chart. The analysis shows this composition is well suited for high school choruses when the bass part is edited to eliminate several A̲'s for the baritones.

More Compositions Analyzed for Range and Tessitura Suitability

Let Nothing Ever Grieve Thee by Brahams. (See Figure 9-5.)

Figure 9-5

Composition __Let Nothing Ever Grieve Thee__   Composer __Brahms_____

Publisher __C. F. Peters_____

Number of beats

soprano		alto		tenor		bass	
a2	-	e2	-1	a1	-1	e1	-
g2	-1	d2	-4	g1	-1	d1	-1
f2	-5	c2	-6	f1	-2	c1	-4
e2	-17	b1	-13.5	e1	-4	b	-6
d2	-19	a1	-10.5	d1	-19	a	-13
c2	-24	g1	-20.5	c1	-22	g	-14.5
b1	-16	f1	-22	b	-29	f	-17.5
a1	-22	e1	-33	a	-12	e	-26.5
g1	-27	d1	-8.5	g	-17	d	-20
f1	-17	c1	-8.5	f	-15	c	-13.5
e1	-6	b	-13	e	-13	B	-7.5
d1	-	a	-	d	-2	A	-7
c1	-	g	-	c	-	G	-
b	-	a	-	B	-	F	-
						E	-4 optional
	__154__		__135.5__		__137__		__134.5__

totals:

Analysis:

The ranges are: soprano, $\underline{e}^{b1} - \underline{g}^2$; alto, $\underline{b}^b - \underline{e}^{b2}$; tenor, $\underline{d} - \underline{a}^{b1}$; bass, $\underline{A} - \underline{d}^1$.

The tessituras are: soprano, $\underline{e}^{b1} - \underline{e}^{b2}$; alto, $\underline{c}^1 - \underline{b}^{b1}$; tenor, $\underline{f} - \underline{d}^1$; bass, $\underline{c} - \underline{a}^b$.

1. The sopranos sing almost 20 beats more than the other parts, but the tessitura and range is acceptable.

2. The alto tessitura is slightly high but should be acceptable later in the year.

3. Tenor tessitura is one step low, also acceptable later in the year.

4. The bass tessitura is good.

5. The tenor's high $\underline{a}^{b1}$ climaxes the composition (see Figure 9-7). The addition of altos to this part could help to bring the music to its esthetic fulfillment. Some of the tenors who have not learned to sing in their upper timbre could remain on $\underline{f}^1$ through beat 2. (See Figure 9-6.)

Figure 9-6   climax from <u>Let Nothing Ever Grieve Thee</u>

Johannes Brahms

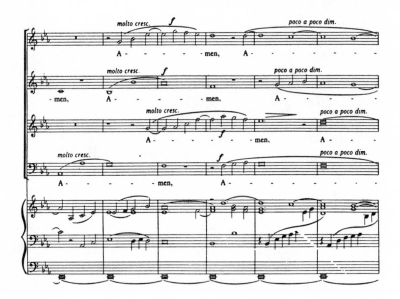

The a^{b1}, g^1 and f^1 in the tenor line must be sung forte for an effective climax. First tenors should sing the line as written; second tenors can sing f^1, g^1, f^1 to relieve straining on the high notes; and altos can be added to the tenor line to fulfill the desired volume. This simple relocation of parts can make the difference in the execution of the composition's climax.

Tenebrae Factae Sunt by Ingeneri. (See Figure 9-7.)

Composition   Tenebrae factae sunt   Composer   Ingegneri

Publisher_____

Number of beats

soprano		alto		tenor		bass	
a2	-	e2	-	a1	-	e1	-
g2	-	d2	-	g1	-	d1	-1.5
f2	-	c2	-	f1	-1	c1	-.5
e2	-	b1	-	e1	-6	b	-4
d2	-7.5	a1	-5	d1	-12	a	-6.5
c2	-10	g1	-4	c1	-9	g	-4
b1	-9	f1	-19.5	b	-7	f	-15
a1	-14.5	e1	-12	a	-14	e	-6
g1	-9.5	d1	-7.5	g	-2	d	-7
f1	-21	c1	-16	f	-4	c	-3.5
e1	-5	b	-8.5	e	-	B	-2
d1	-3	a	-3	d	-	A	-2
c1	-2	g	-	c	-	G	-
	82		75.5		55		54

totals:

Figure 9-7

Analysis:

The ranges are: soprano, $\underline{c}^1 - \underline{d}^1$; alto, $\underline{a} - \underline{a}^1$; tenor, $\underline{f} - \underline{f}^1$; bass, $\underline{A} - \underline{d}^1$.

The tessituras are: soprano, $\underline{f}^1 - \underline{c}^2$; alto, $\underline{c}^1 - \underline{f}^1$; tenor, $\underline{a} - \underline{c}^1$; bass, $\underline{c} - \underline{a}$.

All four parts check favorably with the singer's tessitura chart. No changes are required—a case of excellent music whose notes fall within the acceptable limits of high school voices. There are plenty more like this, if we dig hard enough.

"Hallelujah" from *Messiah* by Handel. (See Figure 9-8.)

Composition _____Hallelujah (Messiah)_____   Composer _____Handel_____

Publisher _____Generally available_____

Number of beats

soprano		alto		tenor		bass	
a2	-1	f2	-	a1	-1.5	e1	-
g2	-14	e2	-	g1	-16.5	d1	-33
f2	-25.5	d2	-2	f1	-32	c1	-15
e2	-33.25	c2	-	e1	-17	b	-17.5
d2	-94	b1	-18	d1	-70.5	a	-40
c2	-20	a1	-108	c1	-16.5	g	-32
b1	-9	g1	-23	b	-21	f	-35.5
a1	-50.5	f1	-37.5	a	-47	e	-16
g1	-2.5	e1	-21	g	-9	d	-57.5
f1	-3.5	d1	-36	f	-3.5	c	-4.5
e1	-3	c1	-7.5	e	-3.5	B	-2
d1	-16	b	-8.5	d	-11.5	A	-7
c1	-	a	-.5	c	-	G	-.5
b	-	g	-1	B	-	F	-
	274		262		269.5		261

totals:

Figure 9-8

Analysis:

The ranges are: soprano, $\underline{d}^1 - \underline{a}^2$; alto, $\underline{g} - \underline{d}^1$; tenor, $\underline{d} - \underline{a}^1$; bass, $\underline{g} - \underline{d}^1$.

The tessituras are: soprano, $\underline{a}^1 - \underline{f}^{\#2}$; alto, $\underline{d}^1 - \underline{a}^1$; tenor, $\underline{g} - \underline{f}^{\#1}$; bass, $\underline{d} - \underline{d}^1$.

1. Soprano, tenor and bass tessituras are too high.

2. The composition is relatively long (about 270 beats), making matters worse.

3. This composition is not recommended for average high school voices.

How much does this system limit our repertory? Quite a bit, of course. But I believe the health of young voices is more important than the literature we do. Great choral literature abounds. Handel's *Messiah* is a great work, but should be done only by mature voices and/or voices who have advanced in their vocal technique. There are innumerable compositions of great stature and esthetic value within the limitations set forth in this chapter. It seems a high school chorus could get along fine without Handel's *Messiah*.

Multi-part Music

There are two kinds of music with more than four parts: those in which first and second parts have equal range and tessitura, and those in which second parts have a lower range and tessitura than first parts.

Multi-part music of *equal* parts increases range and tessitura problems, but *unequal* munti-part music solves some of them. With the latter you can assign students a part that more closely fits their individual maturation.

Dynamic Considerations

Dynamics include both volume (loud and soft) and intensity (energy). Dynamic scope is the range of volume; that is, from piano to forte. Dynamic intensity implies the degree of emotion within a particular volume. For example, a shout or a whisper can be emotionally relaxed or emotionally intense. Intensity in performance grows out of mental involvement in aural image; physical tension results when intensity is "put into music."

The quantity of sound that neither requires forcing nor restraint is the best for beginning singers (mezzo-forte). Mezzo-forte varies with individuals relative to maturation, innate ability, and training. In terms of speech, mezzo-forte is the easy speech; forte is a loud speech; piano is a soft shout. It takes more imagination to speak loudly and softly with freedom, since the tendency is to physically push loud speech and physically pull back soft speech.

Dramatic music—oratorios, operatic choruses, many nine-teenth-century works such as Brahm's *Requiem*, etc., cause young singers to push beyond their dynamic range. These works should be left for more mature voices. I hear high schoolers sing solo literature at competition festivals that college voices majors sing only in their junior and senior years. Ask yourself, is the price of doing such music worth it?

Guidelines:

1. Study the volume level and intensity of each composition.
2. The composition that is piano or forte throughout more easily tires young voices than compositions with varying degrees of dynamic levels.
3. Soft singing when devitalized causes vocal strain.
4. Dramatic compositions should be used sparingly.
5. Start each year with music that can be sung effectively without dynamic extremes. Extend the dynamics as the year progresses, as timbres become more pure and the technique of overlapping timbres is learned.

Rhythmic, Intervallic and Tonal Considerations

A piano teacher starts his students on rudimentary material. He teaches counting, fingering, one hand at a time, etc. Band students have years of work in fundamentals of counting and intonation on easier pieces before they try difficult music. Singers need similar training. Choristers, with little or no instrumental background, are asked to sing intricate polyphony, nineteenth-century harmonies, syncopated rhythms, etc. Many young teachers fail because they select music that's too difficult in the beginning of the year. Sometimes they over-estimate the chorus because it did such "great things" in last year's spring concert. Start easy—better to be too easy than too hard. Teach fundamentals and tone concepts in the fall; the springtime will reward you.

Guidelines:

1. Start each year on simple music containing the following limitations:

Rhythm –   𝅝 𝅗𝅥 ♩ ♫

Melody—tonal skips.

Harmony – I – IV – V; gradually add other tonal harmonies.

2. Give the group music it can learn quickly. Early success is important.

3. Teach one or two more difficult numbers in the beginning of the year, mostly by rote.

4. Use a graded repertory (easy to difficult) throughout the year.

5. Have frequent performances—a short fall program or assembly, a Christmas concert, a midwinter concert, a pop concert or light musical, and a spring concert. Below is a suggested repertoire which illustrates how a graded program might be set up.

A Graduated Repertoire Based on Range, Tessitura, Dynamic Intensity, Rhythm, Melody, And Harmonic Considerations

Fall Repertoire:

Sections from *Youth Sings* by Wright; Robbins Music Corp., publisher.

Steal Away
Comin' Through the Rye
I Got a Robe
Fairest Lord Jesus

Use several others for sightreading.

Comments: The first thing the choristers should do is get a sense of being successful. These songs have rhythms that are easy, have narrow ranges and tessituras, and harmonies limited to I, IV, V, VI. They can be learned and memorized fast. Teach them with as little piano as possible; teach concepts of long and short; begin teaching tone concepts and diction as soon as a couple of songs are learned. Similar collections are available, such as those by Irving Cooper, but they are obviously junior high books. Spirituals arranged by Dett, published by Hall-McCreary, are also excellent beginning materials.

Six Folk Songs—Brahms; Edward B. Marks, publishers.

    I'd Enter Your Garden
    How Sad Flow the Streams
    The Fiddler

Comments: I'd Enter Your Garden—High g's in tenor could be changed to e.
The Fiddler—Baritones could stay on e's to avoid singing too many low a's.

Tenebrae Factae Sunt—Ingegneri (generally available).

Comments: A more difficult polyphonic number with excellent range and tessitura.

Christmas Repertoire:

Riu, Riu Chiu—Spanish Carol; Greenberg, editor. Associated Music Publishers, Inc.

Comments: This work features the bass section in a good range and tessitura, and is a good rhythmic selection.

Selections from the *Oxford Book of Carols*; Oxford University Press, publisher.

    #22 Conventry Carol

#86 In Dulci Jubilo
#30 Sweet Was the Song the Virgin Sang
#182 Lullaby My Liking—Holst
#19 Boars Head Carol
#76 Lo, How a Rose—Praetorius
#71 My Dancing Day

Comments: This is just a sampling of the many fine carols in this book. Many of the carols can be purchased separately.
of the carols can be purchased separately.

For Us a Child is Born—J. S. Bach; Galaxy Music Corp.

Comments: A simple but exciting baroque work. A few high tenor notes can be sung by altos. (See Figure 9-9.) Add "low" tenors to bass, heavy altos to tenor, some sopranos to alto. These two measures could be sung SAB. With a few changes of this kind, the work falls well within safe range and tessitura limits. A strong orchestra accompaniment is available which can be played by woodwinds or combinations. A small ensemble is preferable.

Figure 9-9   from the cantata <u>For Us a Child Is Born</u>

J.S. Bach

Altos move to the tenor line; sopranos move to the alto line; the bass line can be reinforced by second tenors.

Winter Repertoire:

Gloria by Vivaldi; Walton Music Corp., publisher.

Comments: The work is relatively easy. Only chorus V needs minor re-distribution of parts. Be sure you never carry the altos too low when you switch them to tenor notes.

Spring Repertoire:

From *Six Easy Madrigals;* Western Music Company Limited.

All Ye Who Music—Donato
Now Spring in All Her Glory—Arkadelt

Comments: Two good openers for a spring program. The final tenor and alto phrases of the Arkadelt selection can be interchanged. (See Figure 9-10.)

Figure 9-10 **from Now Spring in All Her Glory**

Arkadelt

morn - ing dew, the morn - ing dew.

dew, the morn - ing dew.

   The altos and tenors can easily change vocal parts beginning with
measure 1 beat 3 in the tenor line and measure 2 beat 4 in the alto line.
This interchange of parts creates an excellent tessitura for the tenors
and maintains approximately the same tessitura for the altos.

   Ave Verum—Mozart; any publisher.

Comments: See p.50.

   Christ Is Arisen—Schubert; Alexander Broude, Inc., publisher.

Comments: The tenor tessitura is one step low, but all the notes
below g are marked piano.

   Let Nothing Ever Grieve Thee by Brahms; C.F. Peters,
publisher.

Comments: See P. 145.

   Six Folk Songs—Brahms.

   Awake, Awake
   A House Stands 'neath the Willows' Shade

Comments: These are more difficult than those used in the fall
repertoire. Very nice.

Six Chansons—Hindemith; Associated Music Publishers, Inc.

  The Doe
  The Swan
  Since All is Passing
  In Winter
  Springtime
  Orchard

Comments: The Chansons are beautiful. Musically, they are extremely difficult. All the ranges and tessituras except *Springtime* are ideal. The *Springtime* soprano and tenor tessituras are one-half step high. The cycle challenges the singers' musicianship without taxing their voices. Start the easier ones earlier in the year, but perform them as a group in the *spring repertoire*.

Novelty numbers:

  Father William—Fine
  The Mouse That Gnawed the Oaktree Down—Dello Joio
  Tradi Nuka—Wihtol (some easy divisi)

Comments: Generally good. A few changes will improve their singability. Add folksongs and spirituals to complete the list. Select numbers that are not over-arranged.

The above repertoire is meant to be illustrative. The number of rehearsals per week, age median, experience, and the amount of time spent on stage productions all temper your choices—one way or the other. The fall and Christmas programs could be done by most high school choruses with three or more rehearsals per week. Drop the winter program if necessary or substitute a folksong assembly for it. However, a major work per year with instruments (if possible) can become the year's high point.

Every year your chorus is new. Start the year with easy music. Early in my teaching experience, I tried picking up in the fall where the chorus left off in the spring. It didn't work. Use the *Youth Sings* series by Wright or comparable material to begin each year, no matter how good the chorus was last spring.

Aesthetic Considerations

I have never been able to define great music to everyone's satisfaction. Subjectivity rules in any discussion of esthetics. Suffice it to say, good and bad exist in all musical species.

An aesthetic experience results from complete intuitive and emotional involvement in art. A person concentrates and responds until he himself becomes unimportant; he loses himself. Involvement in music can evoke base emotions or lofty ideals. Much of our popular music has trite words set to trite music and stirs our baser emotions. Art, on the other hand, helps us grow intuitively and spiritually. Aesthetic values to look for:

1. The value of the text—what will it say to the teen-ager? What will it do to him emotionally? Aesthetically?
2. The musical setting—do the rhythmic inflections, melodic contours and tonalities enhance the text? Are they congruous?
3. The inherent worth of the music—based on the structure, continuity, appropriate medium and your personal taste. To experience art is to "know it feelingly." Only when music stays within the teen-agers' vocal limitations can they involve their imaginations enough to have an aesthetic experience.

Social Considerations

Educators realize the role music plays in social adjustment and as a recreational agent. The music educator, therefore, often goes overboard in choosing music that has immediate appeal to both performer and audience—music that is fun. Noble Cain believed: "True musical education follows more closely the cultural values that can be gained only from some kind of musical study which will develop the mind, rather than the box office receipts or the adulation of the school."[4] It does not seem a contradiction to perform music of cultural value while at the same time giving aid to the adolescent in his personality development. Shy or overbearing individuals can profit from the group experience whether or not the music is of cultural value, if a good *esprit de corps* prevails. However, if quality music is selected, the chorus program will be of more value to those participating.

Education Implications

The director: The main emphasis in music selection changes when the importance of range, tessitura and dynamic intensity are recognized. The director's prime concern becomes his students' voices, whether his educational emphasis is esthetic, social, or recreational. The year's choral selections are no longer hit and miss; they have continuity and reason. The musical growth of the young people is reward enough for the extra effort involved.

State Music Lists: The present method of selecting music for state competitions and festivals often ignores the technical considerations in music selection. Difficulty is synonymous with wide range, high tessitura, loud dynamic intensity and even louder climaxes. There is much music that is musically difficult that stays within reasonable technical limitations. (The *Six Chansons* by Hindemith is an excellent illustration of this fact.)

State manuals grade music from easy to difficult. Choruses listed as difficult, with few exceptions, over-extend the limits of high school vocal physiology. Honor and prestige is awarded the director whose chorus acquires top ratings. The mixed chorus lists often not only condone, but encourage high school directors to perform music that exceeds the technical equipment of their choristers.

---

4. Noble Cain, *Choral Music and Its Practice* (New York: Witmark and Sons, 1932), p. 37.

Music can be graded by choral teachers for high school choruses according to the difficulty of the rhythm, the melodic intervals and harmonies, the length of the composition, and the depth of the interpretation. A gradual expansion of range, tessitura, and dynamic intensity without exceeding sound technical limitations is possible. A list compiled in this way develops musicianship through music that is vocally beneficial to the chorister.

College Music Education Programs: Teacher preparation programs need to place more emphasis on understanding adolescent voices. Too much is taken for granted. College choruses concentrate on performing mature works, while they give little attention to works suitable for high schools. Beginning teachers are ill-equipped with high school choral literature and, worse yet, they do not have a clearly defined method of music selection. They revert to entertainment music (operettas and Broadway musicals) for the bulk of their "choral" program. I hope this chapter helps remedy this. If the college teacher wants healthy voices to come to him at the undergraduate level, he has to impart music selection techniques to the future music educators he teaches.

Composers: Contemporary composers have written an abundance of music for high school bands and novices at the keyboard. Most contemporary choral works by composers of any stature are written for mature voices. By doing so, they have ignored a potentially good market in the high school chorus.

Composers once aware of the technical limitations of high school voices and the need for good contemporary music in high schools might be encouraged to use the high school chorus as a medium for their creative output. The recent experiment of hiring full-time composers in public schools is worth attention and praise. Commissioning a composer to compose a work for the chorus is another means of creating interest in the high school chorus.

Publishers: Publishers say they give the director what he wants. The publisher has to meet his expenses and make a profit. High school directors who feel strongly enough about selecting music according to the technical considerations stated herein could demand that the publisher include ranges and tessituras at the beginning of each composition. Any publisher who attempts to clarify these considerations warrants the attention of music educators.

CHAPTER 10

Learning and Interpreting the Score

INSIGHT IS THE goal of learning. We gain insight both by trial and error and by conditioned response to stimuli, which results from analytical and/or intuitive thinking. This chapter includes mastery of the mechanics of the score by empirical and conditioned-response processes, and interpretation of the score through analytical and intuitive thinking. A musician is usually intuitive; that is, he has instant feeling as to how music should go. As he studies melody, rhythm, and harmony, he intuitively senses tempo, mood, dynamics, and phrasing. However, as a teacher-conductor he has to present his intuitive ideas and feelings to his choir through an analytical plan. Though your interpretive ideas come intuitively, the score needs analytical study before you can communicate your ideas to the choir. Therefore, a step-by-step analysis of the text and music checks your intuitive "leaps" and deepens your understanding. Jerome Bruner writes: "Intuition implies the act of grasping the meaning, significance or structure of a problem or situation without explicit reliance on the analytical apparatus of one's craft."[1] Intuition is unquestionably important to the realization

1. Jerome Bruner, *The Process of Education* (New York: Vintage Books, Random House Inc., 1960), p. 60.

of creative interpretation, but . . . "some intuitive leaps are 'good' and some are 'bad' in terms of how they turn out."[2] Thus analytical study of the score complements and supplements intuitive feelings.

Our interpretive goals as teachers and conductors are: (1) an aural mastery of the score—practice until you can "hear" the score in your imagination with accuracy; (2) a sense of the emotional content of the composition; (3) an insight into the meaning *behind* the musical symbols; (4) a plan through which we can transfer our knowledge of and feeling for the text and music to our chorus and, eventually, to our audiences.

Play through a composition on the piano and determine its suitability for high school voices by the techniques presented in Chapter Nine. Interpretation and technical mastery of the score can be accomplished through the following eight steps.

Step 1–Text

The composer began with the text; the interpreter should begin with the text. Word meanings and pronunciations are the basis of all good choral singing and interpretive insights. Rhythm and meter depend on the natural inflections of words, and dynamics result from the intensity, mood, and emotional content of the text. Composers usually place melodic high points at verbal high points. Harmonic tensions highlight the tensions of the words.

Because speech and pitch have different origins in the brain, a singer should develop good speech habits to the same degree he develops tonal memory. Husler and Rodd-Marling write: "We are told that the speech and pitch centres in the brain, though contiguous, are differently located so that if the ability to speak has been lost, singing is still possible and vice versa."[3] We begin

---

2. *Ibid.* p. 60.
3. Frederick Husler and Yvonne Rodd-Marling, *Singing: The Physical Nature of the Vocal Organ*, (London: Octobre House, 1966), p. 96.

the mastery of the score by studying words because the composer's musical ideas grew out of the text and its meaning to him.

Order of textual study:

1. Pronunciation: be sure of the correct pronunciation of each word and the exact sound of each vowel. Autumn sounds o-t m, not ah-tehm, etc.

2. Voiced consonants: b, d and g (as in God), j, g (as in George), s (as in easy), th (as in the), and v are consonants that are voiced. Check all words for these sounds. "God" must not sound "Kod" or "Got;" "times" sounds "timz," not "times;" "leave" must not sound "leaf."

3. Word separation: when the final consonant of a word preceding a key word changes the meaning of the key word, the words are separated:

hit/in, not hittin
more/on, not moron

The secret of successful legato singing in these instances is to sing the vowel on the beat and the consonant before the beat. It is wrong to sing the preceding consonant on the beat. Imagining the vowels on the beat causes separation without a mechanical-sounding execution.

4. Text reading: read the poetry aloud until you sense the natural inflections of the words. Read as though you had an audience. What are the key words of each sentence of each section? What words do you emphasize for emotional impact? What consonants need emotional treatment? What mood does the text create in you? Emphasizing all the consonants to the same extent results in a monotonous, unexpressive performance in which the meaning behind the words is lost, even though each word is distinct.

Example: "Let the people praise Thee, O God"

Here the key words are "people," "praise," and "God." If the audience hears only those three words, they have the meaning of the phrase. Concentrate, then, on the underlined consonants, people praise God, and clarity will be guaranteed. The emotional impact of the words will be amplified. I regret that colleges do not require courses in undergraduate schools that lead to greater insights into poets' use of words, and consequently a more practical implementation of words by us as interpreters.

5. The composer: study the text in light of what you know about the composer and the poetry of his time. How would he have reacted to the text? Would it have been objective or subjective, universal or personal, tame or wild? Throughout his life, J. S. Bach was a Christian, devoted to God. The non-Biblical poetry that he set to music is considered inane and sentimental by many "modern" men, except perhaps 20th century Christians who appreciate it in light of their own faith and experience. The non-Christian appreciates Bach's music but finds it difficult to respond to Bach's text to the same extent. Modern musicians are in a dilemma. As artists they cannot ignore this musical genius. They either have to sense vicariously the depth of feeling Bach had in his Christian faith or perform the music without emotion, destroying the composer's intentions. It seems to me that we need to study a text in light of the composer's philosophic thought and realize his intentions in and through our own imaginative processes and emotional make-up. Step 1 in brief: check the pronunciation of all words, separate words to avoid changes in word meanings, underline key words in the score, and study the text in light of the composer's philosophic presuppositions and the period in which the text was written. Practice reading the text with appropriate inflections. Vary the tempo, dynamics and pitch level of the speaking voice to emphasize the mood and emotional intensity of the text until its full meaning becomes clear.

Step 2—Rhythm

Bars serve two purposes: first, they serve as an aid to the singer in reading music, and second, they show where the recurring accents on the rhythm are. In homophonic music the presence of bars causes few problems. Where bar lines create interpretive problems is in polyphonic music, especially of the 15th, 16th and early 17th centuries. According to Grosvenor Cooper and Leonard Meyer, the bar did not have the same meaning prior to the 17th century. They write: . . . "during the middle ages and the Renaissance there were no bar lines at all."[4]

The relationship and interaction of rhythm and meter in 16th century polyphony remain in a state of controversy. The main elements of the controversy center around the use or disuse of bars and whether or not the rhythmic texture is polyrhythmic or homorhythmic.

Figures 10-1a, 10-1b, and 10-1c show the possibilities of rhythmic interpretation of the first phrase a seventeenth-century setting of *Ein Feste Burg (A Mighty Fortress is Our God).* (See Figures. 10-1a, b and c.) Figure 10-1 includes: first,

A migh - ty for_____ tress is_____ our God.

Figure 10-1a

A migh - ty for_____ tress is_____ our God.

Figure 10-1b

A migh - ty for__ tress is_____ our God.

Figure 10-1c

4. Grosvenor Cooper and Leonard B. Meyer, *The Rhythmic Structure of Music,* (Chicago: The University of Chicago Press, Phoenix edition, 1963), p. 89.

the original rhythm without bars (see Figure 10-1a); second, as it might be barred in a modern edition (see Figure 10-1b); third, a version rebarred according to the natural text inflections (see Figure 10-1c). The poetic meter is simple iambic (∪ —). The two-four meter implies an accent on beat one of measure three (*tress*) and a syncopation on beat two (*is*). Some authorities claim this type of metric treatment is wrong, that rhythmic nuances are governed by text inflection (poetic meter), and that bars should be added accordingly (Figure 10-1c). When this rebarring technique is followed throughout a polyphonic composition, polymeters result. (See Figure 10-2.) The first phrase of the soprano begins with two ternary groupings and then continues in binary groupings until the second phrase. The changes from ternary to binary groupings on different beats in each voice part create a complex rhythmic picture very

Figure 10-2

Make Ye Joy to God   (section C)

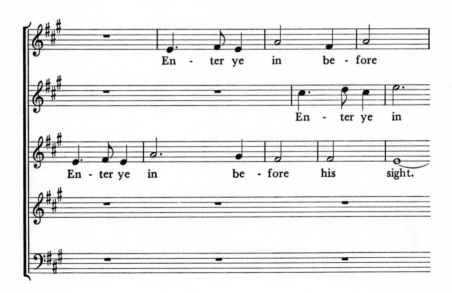

different from the one in which the bars fall simultaneously in all voice parts. Latest research by musicologists indicates that re-barring (as shown in Figure 10-2) is a distortion of the Renaissance style and that syncopation was a true stylistic element of the 16th century. Evidence that composers wrote their original scores with vertical bars has been expounded by Edward Lowinsky.[5]

Whereas the concept of re-barring, as shown in Figure 10-2, is now regarded as being fallacious, a strict vertical interpretation of the metric structure of pre-baroque polyphony results in a performance that lacks the true nature of polyphonic writing; that is, the rise and fall of each voice in imitation of the other voices. Gustave Reese sums up the matter: "Renaissance polyphony was much more elastic in the regular recurrance of its accent than was the music of the baroque, classic and romantic periods, but . . . this elasticity was made manifest with reference to a prevalent meter. The elasticity could result in two ways: (1) the composer could change the actual meter, through the sense of the music itself without changing the time signature, or (2) by an accent producing long or high note at a normally unaccented point in the measure, thus causing a momentary conflict between the macrorhythm and microrhythm." He concludes: "In fact there could be no such conflict in the absence of a macrorhythm with a regularly recurring accent."[6] Robert Donnington's analogy to poetry emphasizes this rhythmic elasticity within a meter: "The regular stresses of the meter, once established, are present in one's mind; the actual stresses of the words partly conflict with them, and in this tacit 'counterpoint' lies much of its beauty."[7]

It seems to me that rhythmic interpretation of 16th century music is best determined through consideration of the following criteria:

---

5. Edward E. Lowinsky, "Early Scores in Manuscript" *Journal of the American Musciological Society*, Vol. XIII (1960), pp. 126-173.

6. Gustave Reese, *Music in the Renaissance* (New York: W. W. Norton, 1954), p 461.

7. Robert Donnington, *The Interpretation of Early Music* (New York: St. Martins 2nd ed., 1967), p. 354.

1. The original notation and time signature: Keep in mind the time beating technique of following a tactus ↑↓ in which the down and up had equal emphasis (unlike our present beat of one *and* two *and*—strong weak, strong weak).

2. The textual accents: Study the textual accents and compare them to the composer's harmonic rhythm and his placement of long notes and/or high pitches. Where they coincide gives us insight to the composer's intentions of rhythmic groupings.

3. Syncopation: Bear in mind that in all music of the latter half of the 16th century, prepared suspensions are syncopated. These were traditionally written at cadences.

4. Imitative ground plans. Study the composer's imitative ground plans. A head-motive starting on pulse one has its imitation starting on pulse one. A texture might be polymetric not only because of binary and ternary groupings, but also because of the imitation itself.

I have used a portion of William Byrd's *In Manus Tuus* to illustrate the above precepts. (See Figure 10-3.) The rhythm of

In Manus Tuas

William Byrd

Figure 10-3

the opening phrase has one binary group followed by three ternary groups. The time signature indicates that the breve (whole note) receives one tactus (equivalent to two beats in our modern counting system). The phrase, ending after the second *Domine*, contains six and one-half tactuses. The decision not to syncopate the sixth note of the phrase was made for three reasons: (1) it is a long note, (2) it is the highest pitch of the phrase, and (3) there is no dissonance.

˘ —˘-˘ - ˘- -˘- ˘ - ˘ ˘- -˘

In manus tuas, Domine, Domine, commendo spiritum meum,

-˘- - -

spiritum meum

Figure 10-4

The poetic meter is irregular. (See Figure 10-4.) The textual accents agree with the rhythmic interpretation given above.

The imitation ground plan shows the alto imitation of the soprano motive following the same binary-ternary groupings. The second subject enters in the tenor voice. The interaction of these motives and their imitative phrases create rich rhythmic and melodic interest. The textual inflections create a panorama of rhythmic accents. In the cadencial material (measures four and five) the composer utilizes syncopations on the 7-6 suspension and builds tensions through the syncopations in the soprano and alto parts. Within this activity, the first subject begins in the bass, not on pulse *three*, as it appears, but on pulse *one*. All imitations start on the same pulse and contain the same groupings as the subject.

Figure 10-4 shows the complexity of the pulse-structure. (See

Figure 10-5

TACTUS	↕↑↕↑↕↑↕↑↕↑↕↑↕↑↕↑↕↑↕↑
S	1□2□1□2 3 1 2 3 1 2 3 1 2 3 1 2 3 1 2 3
A	- - - - 1 2 1 2 3 1 2 3 1 2 3 1 2 3 1 2
T	- - - - - - - - - - - - - - 3 1 2 3 1
B	- - - - - - - - - - - - - - - - - - -
S	1 2 3 1 2 3 1 2 1 2 - - - - 1 2 1
A	1 2 3 1 2 3 1 2 3 1 2 3 1 2 - - -
T	2 3 1 2 1 2 - - 1 2 1 2 3 1 2 3 1
B	- - - - 1 2 1 2 3 1 2 3 1 2 3 1 2

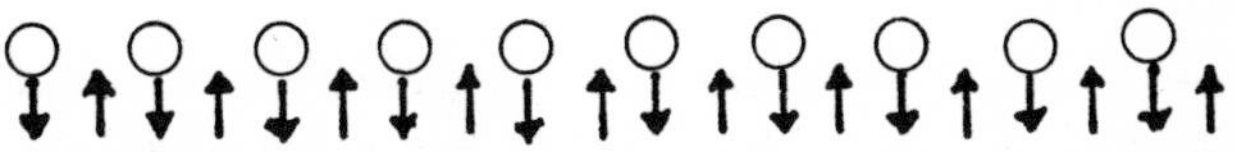

Figure 10-4.) These patterns are not to be thought of as measures. They are performed within a steady, unaccented beat (tactus). To change your beat pattern for each grouping and/or to rebar the rhythm results in musical chaos; teach your singers when to regroup the pulses and when to syncopate.

Conduct these scores with a steady stream of down beats without indicating the regrouping and without the use of traditional beat patterns. Teach the rhythmic flow and accentual independence of the line through text recitation and speech rhythm.

Hemiola

Hemiola is an important feature in vocal music of the baroque period, but was used also by composers of succeeding periods. Hemiola refers to a 3:2 rhythmic ratio. (See Figure 10-5.) The conductor can beat measures three and four as three

Figure 10-6

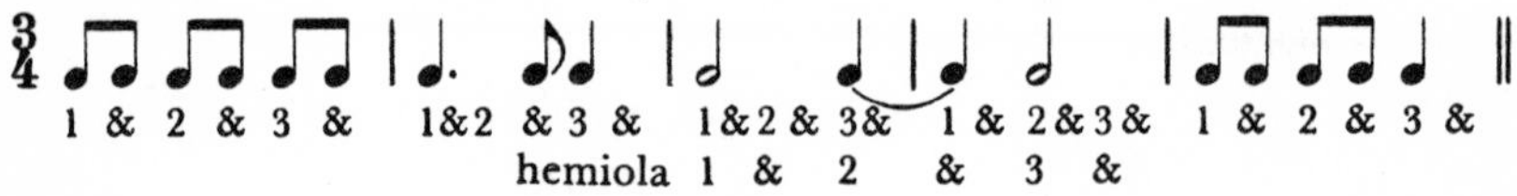

```
1 & 2 & 3 &    1&2 & 3 &   1&2& 3&  1 & 2&3&  1 & 2 & 3 &
                           hemiola 1  &  2   &  3  &
```

measures of two-four, or one measure of three-two. Some conductors keep the three-four pattern while showing the hemiola accents on beat three (as in measure three) and beat two (as in measure four). This method keeps the hemiola measures from losing time. Brahms is well known for his use of *hemiola* technique. Figure 10-6 shows a typical use of *hemiola* by Brahms. (See Figure 10-6.) Another example of *hemiola* is found in Handel's "And the Glory" from *Messiah*. The *hemiola* is in all the orchestra and voice parts except the second violin. (See Figure 10-7.)

from <u>Evening</u> (Der Abend)

Brahms

Figure 10-7

Figure 10-8   **And the Glory**
                                   Handel

Hemiola technique is usually utilized at a cadence; you can 'feel' the
strength that the hemiola gives to the final three measures in the above
example.

Other aspects of rhythmic interpretation, such as *tempo,
rubato, fermata, retardando* and *accelerando*, are presented later
in this chapter, since they are interrelated with melodic and
harmonic considerations as well as textual and rhythmic ones.

Step 3—Melody

Before a conductor steps in front of his chorus he should have sung all the voice parts of each composition he plans to conduct. For a good sight reader, this is an easy task. Everyone should sing all the voice parts, no matter how hard or easy it is for him. In the process, the conductor should follow these steps:

1. Note the difficult intervals in the music. Mark them in the score and mark the important half-steps in scale passages.
2. Note the difficult pitch entrances. Mark the means by which a section can find its pitch following several beats of rest. This can be done by locating a pitch in one of the other voice parts (or in the accompaniment) a beat or two before the difficult entrance. Marking these entrances before you rehearse the composition saves valuable rehearsal time and gains the confidence of your chorus. They appreciate planning! (See Figure 10-8.)

Figure 10-9 from <u>Mass For Mixed Voices</u>

Persichetti

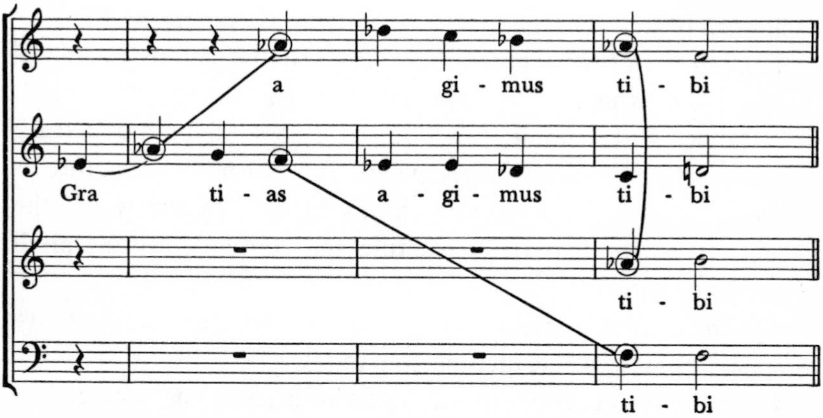

The tenors get their <u>a</u>b by singing silently with the sopranos until the tenor entrance is reached.

3. Decide where to breathe and when to use staggered breathing. Mark in all phase breaths and any places where you do not want a breath where the choir might naturally take one. Decide where staggered breathing is necessary.
4. Determine which voice part has the melody. This is important for balancing the choir.
5. Determine whether the melodic material agrees with your concept of mood and emotional content of the text and rhythm.
6. In polyphonic music, mark where the primary and secondary melodic material is. Each voice part is to be thought horizontally as melody. Mark the prime motives and important entrances in all fugal passages.

Step 4—Harmony

1. Play the composition on the piano for the purpose of getting the vertical structure in your ear, not for interpreting the music. Some play compositions on the piano as the first step to score mastery, but this can be misleading. If you are an accomplished pianist, you will probably end up with a pianistic, non-vocal interpretation. The goal of a conductor is to "hear" the text and music in his imagination as he wants the chorus to sound; you can do this best by approaching the music vocally. Sing it.
2. Mark all harmonic functions at cadences, in modulatory passages, and any passages where the harmonic structure is vague. This helps anticipate chords that might throw off the security of the harmonic structure and consequently the pitch and intonation.
3. Circle all dissonances in the score, including suspensions, appogiaturas and accented passing tones.
4. Study the chords vertically in terms of chord balancing. Sing from the bass note up and mark the color tones of the chords; note the thirds, sevenths, and dissonant notes. Elizabeth Green notes: "Many beautiful effects may be accomplished by giving

the third of the chord special attention wherever the tone quality is weak or thin."[8]

Once you have completed steps 1-4, practice hearing the composition silently in your imagination until you can hear all the parts simultaneously. At first this is difficult, but each success makes your next try easier. Start training yourself on easy music, just as you start training your chorus on easy music. Learning to imagine a composition in the mind is a practical technique, one that all conductors of all ensembles work to achieve. It is said that Toscanini could look at a score at sight and hear the music exactly as it should sound. He was born with the capacity for this, but the ability was developed over a period of many years. See your improvement in perspective. If you begin now to learn scores with this goal in mind, there is no telling how proficient you can be in five to ten years. Compare your progress only with yourself, never with others.

Step 5—Phrasing And Phrase Building

The following procedures teach phrasing concepts that have proven valuable to me.

All music except the avant-garde compositions of the 20th century has forward motion (a feeling of coming from a point of tension and going to a point of tension). Western man tends to think of what he is doing in the present in relation to what he did yesterday in planning for tomorrow. Western music of the past reflects this attitude and was written from this philosophic standpoint. Much modern music shows the influence of oriental thought patterns. Live for the moment; each experience is an entity in itself. The "new" sounds should be contemplated by themselves rather than listened in reference to what was before and what is to come. Sounds exist for and by themselves; rhythm is motionless; harmonic and melodic organization is indistinguishable.

---

8. Elizabeth A.H. Green, *The Modern Conductor*, Englewood Cliffs, N.J.: Prentice-Hall, Inc. second ed., 1969), p. 177.

In tonal music, rhythm, meter, melody, and harmony go hand in hand to create forward movement. Interpreters study the organization of these musical elements to discover the points of tension within each phrase and the greatest tension point in the composition (climax). In other words, where is each phrase going and where are the aggregate phrases going?

The phrase is the essence of music. Each phrase tenses and relaxes again and again until it reaches its highest point of tension and final relaxation. The point of greatest tension in a phrase is called crusis; the part of the phrase that leads to the crusis is called anacrusis; and the notes that follow the crusis are called feminine rhythm. The rise and fall of tensions within the anacrusis are called nuances.

Anacrusis, crusis, and feminine rhythm are marked in musical examples as follows:

      anacrusis   crusis   feminine rhythm

To have tension, a note must be set off from other notes in the phrase in some way (if all tones are alike there are no tensions). Tensions result from the following rhythmic, melodic, and harmonic devices.

Rhythmic devices:

1. Agogic accent—an accent affected either by a longer note surrounded by shorter notes or by dwelling on one note longer than indicated in the tempo; for example, *tenuto* notes and delayed beats.
2. Reiterated rhythmic patterns
3. Syncopation
4. Sudden or dramatic rhythmic changes
5. Polyrhythms (2 against 3); polymeters (3/4 in one voice, 4/4 in another voice) and hemiola.
6. Rests

Melodic Devices:

1. High notes are tension notes.

2. Sequence
3. A wide skip or sudden change of direction
4. Disjunct melodies
5. Emphasis on the leading tone or the fourth tone of a scale (tendency tones). Walter Prison wrote: "Melodically . . . the tendency tones set up by the dissonant intervals move in the direction of their tendencies to a point where they are no longer dissonant and no longer have the tendency to move."[9]
6. Reiterated pitch
7. Augmented and diminished intervals
8. Chromatics

Harmonic Devices:

1. Non-harmonic tones: suspensions, appogiaturas, accented passing tones
2. Isolated dissonant chords
3. Modulatory passages and/or sudden key changes
4. Simple major chord preceeded by dissonant chords
5. Deceptive cadences

Composers most often put the tension in vocal music on the key word of a sentence or phrase. However, to decide where high points (cruses) are on the basis of words alone is misleading. First, the composer's choice of a key word might differ from your choice; second, composers of certain periods of music history put more emphasis on overall mood than on individual word content. Prior to Freud, a composer approached a text very differently than a composer of the post-Freudian era.

As a general practice the crusis of a phrase is located toward the end of a phrase, much as the climax is located toward the end of a composition. This will become apparent to you after

9. Walter Piston, *Harmony* (New York: W. W. Norton and Co., Inc., Rev. ed., 1948 p. 139.

you analyze several compositions by the anacrusis, crusis, and feminine rhythm principles. In homophonic music all voice parts reach the phrase high point simultaneously. Polyphonic music sounds right when each melody reaches its high point independent of the other melodies. Usually at a final cadence, the voices come together for a simultaneous high point. (See Figure 10-9.) An example of homophonic phrase leading can be found in Figure 10-10.

Figure 10-10

Homophonic compositions sound:

S

A

T

B

Polyphonic compositions sound:

S

A

T

B

Analysis of Figure 10-10

Causes of each high point (crusis):

      #1—suspension in soprano
      #2—long note in the soprano, suspension in the alto
      #3—suspension in alto
      #4—suspension in soprano
      #5—agogic accent in soprano and alto, suspension in alto
      #6—agogic accent in soprano, suspension in tenor

Phrases #3, #4 and #5 are excellent examples of phrase building; #5 builds on #4, #4 builds on #3. The phrase building culminates on the word "breaking" (the climax).

Phrase leading and rhythmic nuance properly interpreted provide *polyphony* with a rich panorama of sound unsurpassed by the beauty of chromatic harmony. (See Figure 10-11.)

Figure 10-11

from <u>Break Forth O Beauteous Heavenly Light</u>

J. S. Bach

Example of homophonic texture, with arrows showing high points and climax. Each high point is numbered.

Analysis of Figure 10-11

Causes of each high point:

> soprano #1—agogic accent and the pull of the minor third melodic interval
>
> alto #1—agogic accent and the minor third melodic interval

tenor #1—agogic accent and dissonance against alto
bass #1—agogic accent and the minor third melodic interval

soprano #2—dissonance against the alto $\underline{g}^1$ (augmented fourth)
alto #2—suspension
tenor #2—dissonance against the alto
bass #2—$\underline{d}^b$ is a tendency note which must be resolved in this style of music
soprano #3—agogic accent and melodic minor third
alto #3—agogic accent and melodic minor third

soprano #4—rhythmic stress caused by a change from 6/4 in the previous measures to a feeling of 3/2
alto #4—suspension

The climax is on the first beat of the final measure. Each phrase should build on the previous phrase until the final tension. You can see by the graph in Figure 10-12 a wonderful intertwining of the rise and fall of independent phrase leading. Some phrases are building while others are tapering.

from Call To Remembrance   **Figure 10-12**
Farrant

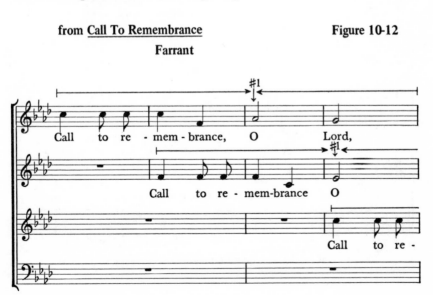

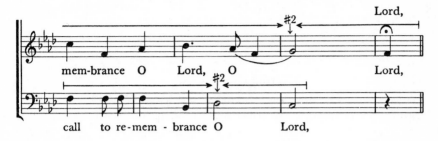

Example of polyphonic music showing the high points of each phrase.

Figure 10-13

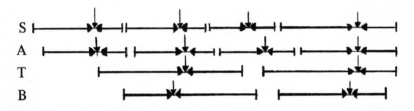

The above graph shows the phrase highpoints in the first section of Farrant's motet *Call To Remembrance*.

Nuances ebb and flow throughout each anacrusis. Melodic and rhythmic inflections must not be pushed aside while the phrase builds to its crusis. The phrase leads to its high point of tension with little tensions and relaxations (nuances) along the way.

Step 6—Dynamics

How loud is a marked *forte*? How soft should a *piano* sound? Dynamics are determined by the mood and intensity of the text, by the composer's dynamic markings, and then tempered by the style of the music (romantic or classic). These factors influence the pre-existing markings and our interpretation of a score that does not have dynamics. Other dynamic considerations are:

1. *Phrasing*: Phrase leading (anacrusis) implies crescendo, but the crescendo must stay within the dynamic panel suggested by the composer or determined by your text analysis when no composer's dynamic marks exist. (See Figure 10-13.) Only in dramatic moments should you crescendo more than one dynamic panel within a phrase. If a crescendo is indicated, follow the dynamic plan of the composer—in any case a phrase requires forward motion. The only time one does not increase the intensity of a phrase is when the composer deliberately requests a static effect or forces a long diminuendo on his music, or as previously stated, in *avant garde* music.

Figure 10-14

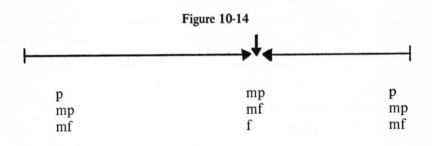

p	mp	p
mp	mf	mp
mf	f	mf

Dynamic Panels:

piano	mezzo-forte	forte
mp	f	ff
p	mf	f
pp	mp	mf

2. *Phrase building*: The second phrase should be no more than one dynamic panel louder than the preceding phrase unless indicated by the composer or for an affectation.

3. *Balance*: Voice parts are usually balanced by adjusting the dynamics of each section. The melody in a homophonic composition needs more presence than the harmony. If your soprano section has the melody and this is your strongest section (so often the case), then no problem exists. But when the melody is in another voice you do have a problem of balance. Having one part sing *mf* while the others sing *mp* is one solution. Another is to change some voices from one part to another—high tenors and second sopranos can sing with the altos, altos and high baritones can help the tenors, second tenors can bolster a high bass part, etc.

4. *Sometimes crescendo and diminuendo wedge-markings* are placed within a phrase without specific reference to the exact beat on which the phrase climaxes. The exact placement of each crusis is left to the musical judgment of the interpreter. *Always continue a crescendo through the crusis before diminishing, no matter where the dynamic wedge-markings are placed on the score.*

The dynamic markings in the Bach example (Figure 10-10) are based on the dynamic considerations in this chapter. The *mf* in the first phrase is my preference between *mf* and forte. The repeated phrase is treated as an echo phrase. It should be only one dynamic panel softer than the first phrase—any more contrast would be affectation. Measures #3, #4, and #5 are dynamically terraced. This is a good example of how phrase building and dynamic design interrelate. (Another plan could be #3 *mp;* #4 *mf;* #5 *f.*) The *p* in phrase #6 is an intentional affectation to contrast the words with those of phrase #5. Some interpreters might feel this is too much contrast and prefer to start phrase #6 *mf* and taper to *p* only on the final fermata. I have not inserted crescendo or diminuendo marks; the phrase leading will cause sufficient volume increase and decrease.

The dynamic level of the Farrant is primarily *mf*. The phrases should rise and fall within this dynamic panel, with a slight increase in intensity on each phrase until a forte level is reached at the climax. Depending on the interpreter, the design could be primarily *p* with a *mf* on the climax. The second soprano and alto phrases could be treated as echo phrases and sung one panel softer. The soprano's tessitura is low and will sound softer without a dynamic indication.

Step 7—Tempo

Harry Robert Wilson writes: "The conductor, in the final analysis, must resort to the inherent quality of the music for the most effective tempo."[10] Tempo can be determined by discovering the intrinsic qualities of a composition. The following considerations help unfold the inherent qualities of a composition:

1. *Text*: the general mood of the text should be the key to your final tempo. This is then tempered by the period in which the music was written and your knowledge of the composer.

2. *Texture*: according to Kurt Adler, thin texture implies a faster tempo; thick texture, a slower tempo. He writes: "A monophonic setting will be taken faster than a complicated polyphonic setting of the same melody."[11]

3. *Harmonic rhythm:* frequent harmonic changes imply a slower tempo than music that has one harmony per measure.

4. *Density of harmony:* rich-sounding chromatic chords often imply a slower tempo.

5. *Text setting:* the number of notes per word or words per beat influence tempo. Melismatic sections are often sung faster

10. Harry Robert Wilson, *Artistic Choral Singing* (New York: G. Schirmer, Inc., 1959), p. 54.

11. Kurt Adler, *The Art of Accompanying and Coaching* (Minneapolis: The U. of Minnesota Press, 1965), p. 114.

than passages where there is a word for every note in the melody.

External considerations that influence tempo choices:

1. The size of the chorus: small choirs sound better on slightly faster tempos; large ones on slower tempos. Breathing also influences tempo; a large group can more effectively stagger breathing in long, slow phrases.
2. The acoustics of a hall: a "live" hall requires a slower tempo; a dry hall, a faster tempo.
3. The technical proficiency of the choir: sustained singing is very difficult for beginning choirs, and coloratura is impossible. The tempo must be adjusted to the technique of the group.
4. Adler writes on tempo: "Our principle tempo indications—allegro, allegretto and andante—are based on the Affektenlehre [affectations, musical tone painting] which in baroque times gained more and more popularity. Allegro means gay; andante walking. These were character indications and not simply indications of tempo like adagio and presto."[12] If andante is a walking tempo, then each conductor's andante tempo will be influenced by his age, size, and temperament (how fast he walks, etc.). How gay is allegro? This depends also on the conductor's experiences and emotional makeup.
5. Metronome markings placed in the music by a composer deserve some attention. My rule of thumb? Be sure to have excellent reasons based on score study and the above tempo considerations before tampering with them.
6. Accelerando (speeding up) and ritardando (slowing down) have one rule which governs them—the tempo changes are gradual. Look at the first and last note of the accelerando or ritardando and decide how fast the last note is to be sung, and guide the increase or decrease of speed accordingly. In other words, the final note or notes help us judge the degree of

---

12. *Ibid.* p. 118.

speeding up or slowing down. Some conductors *change* the tempo at the beginning of a ritardando or accelerando. This should be avoided.

Step 8—Expressive Styles: Legato, Tenuto, Staccato, Marcato, and Rubato

A sad difference between orchestral playing and choral singing is the extent to which expressive styles are heard in orchestral performances and the scarcity of them in choral performances. Choral conductors often mold the music to conform to their taste. A fine orchestra will "sound" like Brahms or Mozart. To achieve a Mozart sound the conductor adjusts the instrumentation of his orchestra, the size of the group, the intensity of vibrato, the dynamic compass, the amount of swell on *tenuto*, the crispness of *marcato*, the heaviness of the *staccato*, etc. Singers sometimes fail to concern themselves with these details at all.

The bulk of choral literature has no style markings in the score and composers prior to the nineteenth century left much of the interpretation up to singers. (Often the composer himself served as conductor.) How can we decide when to sing legato or *marcato*? Each composition is a personality in itself and needs to be studied in relation to its text, texture, melody, harmony, and rhythm.

Guidelines:

1. *Legato*: legato is smoothness of musical line. It can be compared to the flow of water from the faucet. The consonants cause slight delays between the vowels like a finger quickly moving back and forth across the steam of water—the flow never stops. There can be no swell (crescendo) on each note, or any diminuendo after the attack.

True legato is impossible for singers who do not sing with freedom and instant release of tone. If they grab physically at the beginning of each tone they destroy a legato line. Consonants do not ruin smooth singing if consonants are instantly released and the vowels are mentally sustained without swelling or fading.

The first phrase of The Swan (*Un Cygne*), from *Six Chansons* by Hindemith is an exquisite example of legato writing. Any swelling (*tenuto*) or accent (*marcato*) destroys the beautiful tone painting of a swan gliding on the water. I prefer a nuance on the word *enfolded*—the soprano followed by the other parts—like a ripple in the water, and then a static phrase to enhance the picture of a slow moving tableau. (See Figure 10-14.)

2. *Marcato: marcato* is a "tossed" accent that sounds **> > >** . It can be sung light or heavy. Tone must begin instantly and be followed by diminuendo for true *marcato* style. It is very effective in contrapuntal music and especially in polyphonic music of baroque composers; *marcato* style clarifies polyphony. A light *marcato* is buoyant; a heavy *marcato* is strong and dignified. Legato and marcato are the bread and butter of most singing, whereas *tenuto* and staccato are the spices.

Without *marcato* some compositions sound muddy. More importantly, the heavy and light marcato treatments help bring out meaning behind text settings.

3. *Tenuto: tenuto* is a pressed accent, a pull and swell after the beat with a slight release in volume just before the next beat. It can be the most beautiful and emotionally effective of the expressive styles. If it is not used sparingly, however, its impact is lost and the music becomes sentimentalized; like candy, too much can make a person sick. Conduct *tenuto* beats by pretending to pull your hand through molasses or by assimilating the bowing of a cello. Feel a relaxation of the arm and hand just before the next beat. The *tenuto* is most effective in music of the 19th century and/or as an expressive device to enhance particular words or phrases. The excerpt from Brahm's *Evening* (Figure 10-6) has several places where *tenuto* could be used (for

Figure 10-15   The first five measures of <u>A Swan</u>
                                                                    Hindemith

A Swan
Un Cygne

Rainer Maria Rilke
English version by
Elaine de Sinçay

For Four-Part Chorus of Mixed Voices
Unaccompanied

Paul Hindemith

Lento (♩ = 60-66)

Soprano

A swan is breast - ing the flow All in him - self _____
Un cy - gne a - van - ce sur l'eau tout en - tou - ré _____

Alto

A swan is breast - ing the flow All in him -
Un cy - gne a - van - ce sur l'eau en - tou - ré

Tenor

A swan is breast - ing the flow All in him -
Un cy - gne a - van - ce sur l'eau en - tou - ré

Bass

A swan is breast - ing the flow All in him -
Un cy - gne a - van - ce sur l'eau en - tou - ré

_____ en - fold - ed Like a slow - mov - ing ta - bleau.
_____ de lui - mê - me com me un glis - sant ta - bleau;

self en - fold - ed, A slow - mov - ing ta - bleau.
de lui - mê - me com me un glis - sant ta - bleau; *mf*

self en - fold - ed, A slow - mov - ing ta - bleau. And so, at some
de lui - mê - me com me un glis - sant ta - bleau, ain - si à cer -

self en - fold - ed, A slow - mov - ing ta - bleau.
de lui - mê - me com me un glis - sant ta - bleau;

A-505

example, the first word in the second phrase in each voice part and the hemiola notes in the soprano, measures five and six).

4. *Staccato*: staccato passages demand complete separation between words—I seldom hear amateur choirs implement this technique. If it is approached mechanically or physically, all kinds of vocal problems crop up; for instance, grabbing at the throat and stomach muscles. The separation of words (staccato) must be imagined in the singers' minds before they attempt to sing aloud. If the choristers can imagine a series of words and pitches legato, *tenuto*, staccato, or *marcato*, they can sing in these styles. Make clear to the singers exactly what you want, then rehearse silently until they can imagine the exact style in their minds before singing aloud. In staccato style, as in all styles, phrase leading should be observed.

5. *Rubato: rubato* is a speeding and slowing of the pulse within a phrase. This too is spice. There is little place for *rubato* in polyphonic music generally, but homophony often never comes alive without this "playing with the beat." *Rubato* makes musical sense only when it is inherent in the text and musical style itself. A good composition never needs gimmicks. There is no way of showing in a musical score how much give and take you should conduct. Your intuitive musicianship does this. If you don't feel *rubato* from within, don't force it from without. The rule for *rubato* is that the overall tempo must not change. One should arrive at the end of each *rubato* section at the same moment he would have had he not "played with the beat." The performer must steal from one note to give more time to another note. There is a speeding up and slowing down within each *rubato* measure or phrase. Too often beginning performers merely execute a ritard when they are attempting *rubato*.

Step 9—Fermata

A *fermata* or hold indicates a non-rhythmic elongation of a tone. There are four kinds of *fermata:*

1. The breath *fermata:* this type is found in chorales and hymns (A Mighty Fortress, etc.) and it indicates a phrase—no elongation. It is not a *fermata* in the modern sense.
2. The moving *fermata*: the hold and the next note are connected.
3. The stopped *fermata*: the reflex of the cutoff serves as the preparation for the next note.
4. The pause *fermata*: come to a complete stop—pause—conduct the preparatory beat—conduct the next note.

Refer to the Bach choral, *Break Forth O Beauteous Heavenly Light*, on page 183 of this chapter.

1. The first *fermata* is a breath *fermata*—no elongation. Take a quick breath and sing on.
2. The second *fermata* is a stopped *fermata*—the note is slightly lengthened; the reflex of the cutoff gesture is the preparation for the next beat. Be sure the preparation is in tempo.
3. The third, fourth and fifth *fermatas* are phrase indications—no elongation.
4. The final *fermata* is slightly elongated. Be sure to conduct a preparation before the cutoff.

Guidelines:

1. On *fermatas* that merely indicate a breath, mark in a rest indicating precisley the length of the breath.
2. On moving *fermatas*, sustain the hold and continue without a stop. A half preparation is needed to alert the choir to the fourth beat. Figure 10-16a shows how to conduct a moving fermata on beat three of a four-four measure.
3. On stopped *fermatas*, the reflex of the cutoff serves as the preparation. Be sure the preparatory beat is in tempo. (See Figure 10-16b.)
4. On pause *fermatas*, after the reflex of the cutoff the hand

Figure 10-16 a

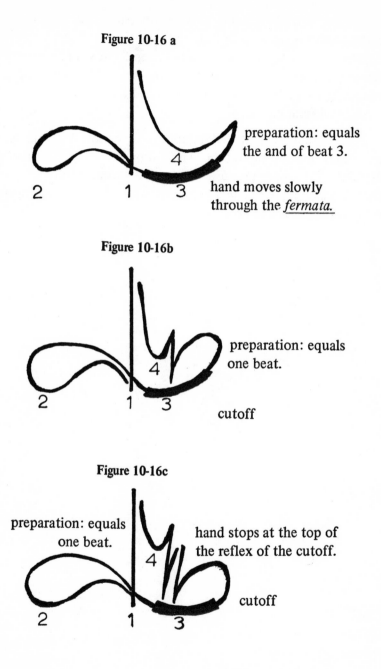

preparation: equals
the and of beat 3.

hand moves slowly
through the *fermata.*

Figure 10-16b

preparation: equals
one beat.

cutoff

Figure 10-16c

preparation: equals
one beat.

hand stops at the top of
the reflex of the cutoff.

cutoff

comes to a stop. There is a silent pause followed by a preparation for the next beat. (See Figure 10-16c.)

5. The *fermata* technique you use depends on your interpretation of the emotional content of the text and your musical taste. Each *fermata* needs to be examined within the context of mood, style and period.

This chapter has included an approach to score learning and guidelines for interpretation. The following chapter includes methods for communicating the score from conductor to student, and rehearsal techniques valuable to good rehearsal attitudes and learning processes.

CHAPTER 11

Rehearsing the Score with the
High School Chorus

Your Relationship With Your Singers

1. Set goals for your choristers. You know philosophically why you are in the position you are and what you hope to achieve. Share your dreams with your singers so they too can sense the excitement of reaching out for something beyond themselves.
2. Demand self-discipline. Help your singers become motivated to the place that they work hard in rehearsals because they want to improve—not just because you make them. At first the conductor's discipline might be necessary to bring order out of chaos. Proper encouragement helps a young person become more involved in the group. As he begins to realize the potential of his chorus, he begins to take it upon himself to be more attentive. A chorus in which all the singers are aggressive without reaching the goals placed before them is an excellent one indeed.
3. Put individuals above performances. Young people quickly discern whether a director loves them and cares about their progress as singer-musicians or uses them to glorify himself in performances. We teach because we are needed by young

people. We teach voice because singing is an integral part of the whole personality. Those who learn to sing better become more complete human beings. We teach choral music because a choral organization is an excellent place to teach voice, and choral music enriches the lives of the participants spiritually, aesthetically, and socially.

4. Respect your singers as people. Respect their capabilities and understand their personal and environmental limitations. Enjoy your choristers as human beings with all that the term implies.

5. Set high standards. Know what you and your group are capable of doing and do it well. However, never destroy your personal relationship with people in an effort to reach goals beyond your or their potential. If you begin to resent your chorus because they do not reach your standards, remind yourself of your own weaknesses even after years of specialized training.

6. Respect your young people in every way. Respect your own achievements—respect theirs.

7. Be objective. Many conductors fail because they take every discipline problem and wrong note personally. You have a job to do. You know how to do it, so do it. Do your job and let the "chips fall where they may." A poor rehearsal can be caused by innumerable factors outside of your control.

Don't get personally involved in your students' problems. A psychiatrist is effective because he does not get emotionally involved in the problems his patients reveal. If he did, the patient could no longer look to him for strength and guidance. The lack of objectivity in a teacher-pupil relationship has been the downfall of many teachers and conductors.

8. Be professional. Know your professional tools completely and implement them. Do not try to be mother, father, pastor, psychologist and friend to your students. Be what you are—a music teacher—and be a good one. The young people will like you much more for it and look to you for the guidance and direction you can give best—that of a vocal music authority.

9. Compliment your choirs, but be honest. It is honest to praise progress; it is dishonest to tell a group they have achieved more than they really have.

10. Have fun in rehearsals. Laugh when impromptu funny things happen, especially when the joke is on you. Do not use rehearsal time to show off your joke-telling ability; don't use your rehearsals as a soap box to air your views.

11. Beware of idiosyncrasies that annoy your chorus. Clapping hands to stop the chorus, snapping fingers or tapping the baton on the stand to keep time, and excessive foot-tapping are annoying habits. Tape record some of your rehearsals to check against faults that might grate on your singers' nerves.

12. Demand 100 percent attendance and promptness at rehearsals. Nothing demoralizes a group more than poor attendance and tardiness. If the student is in school, he should be in chorus. If he can't sing because of a sore throat, he can learn notes and rhythms.

Your Rehearsal Plans

1. Have the rehearsal room ready. Set up risers, chairs, etc., before the singers come into rehearsals. Have your rehearsal schedule written on a blackboard. Music can be passed out as the singers come into the room.

2. Plan every rehearsal carefully. Too often conductors don't have enough rehearsal time because they don't make full use of the time they have. Know exactly how many minutes you can spend on each number from the beginning of the year to your first program and from program to program. Then schedule exactly how many minutes you will spend on each number in a single rehearsal. In the heat of the rehearsal time, adjustments can be made. After each rehearsal, estimate how much actual time you spent on each number (or have a student keep a log for you). Plan the next rehearsal accordingly.

3. Vary your rehearsal plans. Start some rehearsals with

familiar compositions, some with rhythmic drill, some with speaking, etc. Stay out of a rut. Plan to introduce a new vocal technique each week of your first semester of rehearsals. Drill and review. Include in each rehearsal a variety of musical styles and tempos.

4. Teach principles. Plan some time during each rehearsal to teach a new principle or to reinforce one already taught.

5. Have your chorus stand in rehearsals. Plan to have your chorus stand a good part of each rehearsal. Singers stand in performance; they should stand in rehearsals. Standing posture is somewhat different from seated posture (see Chapter Six). Singers who have rehearsed in a seated position and perform in a standing posture sometimes grow dizzy and even faint. The change in breath pattern causes the blood to rush to the head. If rehearsals are 50 minutes or less, have the chorus stand all the time. This is part of their conditioning as singers.

6. Plan to rehearse in the auditorium, where your group performs, as often as the auditorium schedule allows.

7. Plan all extra rehearsals ahead of time. Give your singers ample time to plan for any extra rehearsals you may schedule. Mimeograph a rehearsal schedule and pass it out in the beginning of your preparation for the next concert. Remember, it is always easier to subtract time than to add it.

8. Show consideration to your accompanist. Give new music to your accompanist at least one week prior to the rehearsal of that number.

9. Let your officers participate. You alone are responsible for selecting the music that the chorus rehearses and you alone are responsible for teaching it. Your officers can plan social functions, help recruit new members, and help with the physical aspects of the organization; for example, moving risers and setting up risers and chairs for special rehearsals.

10. Make a standing or seating chart prior to your first rehearsal. Mimeograph it and have it handed out to each chorus

member as they enter the rehearsal room. Any future seating arrangements should be handled in the same manner.

11. Plan to begin and end rehearsals promptly. Begin your rehearsals on time, whether everyone is in his place or not. Ask your choristers to show you the courtesy of being "ready to go" when the bell rings. On the other hand, show them the courtesy of stopping rehearsals on time. Nothing frustrates choristers more than those extra minutes after the bell when we keep going. Make a deal. You let the chorus out on time if they start on time, and keep your end of the bargain.

Teaching Musicianship

1. The basis of muscianship is rhythm. Rhythm is both an intellectual and an emotional-physical stimulus. Few choristers, aside from those with a sound instrumental training, can count rhythms. I believe that the choral conductor and voice teacher have the same responsibility to teach counting to students as the band directors.

a. Rhythm can be taught. First, place a rhythmic drill on the blackboard. (See Figure 11-1.) Think each beat as a down-up

Figure 11-1

beat: ↓ ↑ ↓ ↑ ↓ ↑	↓ ↑ ↓ ↑ ↓ ↑	↓ ↑ ↓ ↑ ↓ ↑	↓ ↑ ↓ ↑ ↓ ↑
count: 1 & 2 & 3 &	1 & 2 & 3 & a	1 e & a 2 e & a 3 &	1 & 2 & 3 &
or say: ta ta ta ta ta	ta ta ta ta	ta ta ta ta ta ta ta ta ta	ta

movement ↓↑ (each arrow represents one-half beat). Draw arrows above or under the pitches to show how the notes coincide with the beats. Have your chorus tap one hand (down-up) on the thigh and say the rhythm on *tah*. Make the down-up (↓↑) movement precise. Each gesture is exactly the same in duration. Set a metronome at the speed of the eighth notes. Hands move down on the click (not before)—and up on the click (not before). After they can do this efficiently, teach them to count the rhythms by saying one and, two and, etc.

b. Before you sing a new number, have your chorus mark the arrows in the music and practice counting (use easy music). Then have them sing the pitches while they count (one and two and). Learn each succeeding new song by singing the pitches on one and two and three and, etc. The intellectual aspect of rhythm and physical coordination becomes secure as the year progresses. You will reap rewards as your singers become better musicians as well as better singers. Don't sell your singers short—teach them to count.

c. Rhythm is movement. Physically moving to rhythm (stepping or dancing the rhythm) helps students feel the rhythmic nuances and musical phrases. Use the eurhythmic approach to physical, rhythmic response. Make all primary beats upward movements from a bent knee position, the values between the primary beats stepped movements. (See Figure 11-2.) Make all

Figure 11-2   **Eurhythmic movements:**

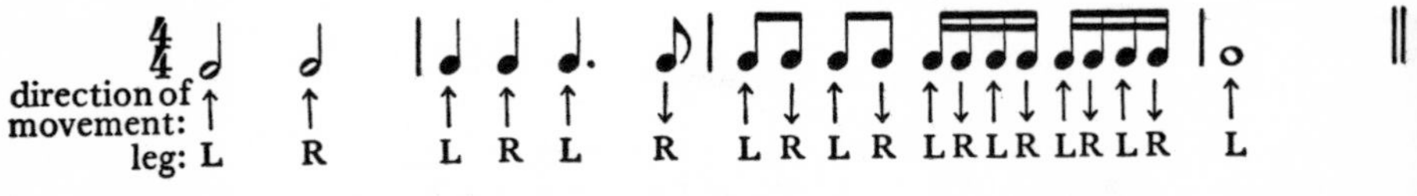

The arrows indicate the direction of each movement. The letters L and R indicate which leg makes each movement. Up arrows refer to a lift movement; down arrows indicate a step movement.

movements graceful. Be sure the movements are up and down (vertical) rather than from side to side (horizontal). These movements can be done in a limited area—and even on standing risers. For variety, stand your chorus in a large circle, leaving as much room between each singer as possible. Practice the movements while counting the rhythms, while reciting the text, and while singing.

Teach rhythms such as the ♩. ♪ ♩. ♪ pattern by this method. Notice the pull through the long note and the toss away feeling of the short note. I have had teachers describe this feeling many times, but I never experienced it until I "danced" it. This is rhythmic nuance experienced.

2. Develop your choristers' tonal memory. I have always contended that a good tonal memory is more important to a chorister than sight reading ability. Tonal memory can be developed through practicing silent singing. Silent practice, more than any other technique, forces singers to be musically independent. Without silent practice, the weaker choristers spend their time listening to and following the stronger musicians.

3. Teach sight-singing in every rehearsal. Sight-singing combines rhythmic and intervalic recognition. Counting, because it is a precise logical science, can be learned by anyone. Recognition of intervals is an intuitive process dependent upon aural memorization of pitch relationships. Some aspiring musicians find it relatively easy to develop pitch relationships; others find it extremely difficult.

a. To improve sight-singing technique, first teach that which can be taught logically—rhythm, and second, guide the singers through reading experiences that will help them learn pitch relationships. The intuitive grasp of pitch relationships cannot be learned if the students are struggling to keep their place in the composition. Hence rhythm is taught first.

b. Our job is to force singers to keep their eyes on the vocal line and force them to trust their inner ears in determining the distance of the step or interval. Make constant reference to the notes on the page, such as: those are steps, you sang skips—that's a wide interval—that note is the same as the one we just sang, but an octave higher. Follow the melodic contour, take a chance, trust your ear—don't be afraid of making mistakes.

c. Start the year's program with very easy music and gradually feed the chorus more difficult intervals and harmonies. Read through some very easy compositions silently several times before singing aloud. It is surprising sometimes how well the chorus does.

d. Reading music with *one and two and,* etc., throughout compositions forces students to glue their eyes on the notes. This technique more than any other gives the choral singers a chance to recognize and memorize aural relationships.

e. Use your accompanist as sparingly as possible, but don't let the singers on their own so much that they become discouraged. If, for example, your altos read well, have this part omitted from the piano score. If the basses are particularly weak, have their notes played while the others sing unaccompanied. Vary your music presentation so the choristers will never get bored. Make them think for themselves as often as possible and in every way you can.

4. Teach phrasing. You have analyzed each composition and have determined the musical phrasing of each score. Share your knowledge of phrasing with your students. Show the high points of each phrase on a blackboard and share with them the musical and textual reasons for each high point. Demonstrate how a phrase should be sung from anacrusis to its crusis and feminine resolution. Take time to "draw" phrases ——➤ ↓◄—— in the score of at least one short composition. After this experience, your directions about high points, phrase leadings, and resolutions will make sense. Our high school singers are musical novices who do not know how music goes until we tell them.

5. Perform music from memory and with music. Choruses that perform everything from memory give the impression of having learned all their notes by rote. The days of singing everything

from memory are over. Compositions that are memorized in the course of learning them should be sung from memory. Otherwise, use music and teach your singers to read notes.

6. Sing both accompanied and unaccompanied music. The *a cappella* tradition no longer exists except in a relatively small circle. The music available with accompaniment is just as vast and exciting as the *a cappella* literature. Don't limit your singers' experience to any one style. Give them the experience of singing with piano, organ, guitar, orchestra, strings alone, winds alone, and unaccompanied.

7. Perform a repertoire that includes music that is sacred and secular, slow, fast and moderate, of different textures (polyphony, homophony and monophony), music of all periods including medieval and contemporary music, music with great texts and music with humorous texts. Give your choristers the complete and meaningful experience that music can give them. Every aspect of human behavior is expressed in music. Every emotion and every human experience can be found in texts set to music.

Teaching The Score

1. Select music that you believe in and love. Beside the technical considerations outlined in Chapter Nine, it is important that you love the music you ask your chorus to rehearse and perform. Your love for the music rubs off on those you conduct. Never do music merely because the young people want to do it or to impress your colleagues. Choose music you enjoy and the chorus and audience will enjoy it with you.
2. Know the musical score thoroughly before you begin rehearsing it. No matter what your tastes are, know the score *before* you rehearse it with your singers. You will be more efficient and free to be a more creative conductor and a better voice teacher.

3. Begin each composition in the tempo you want to perform it. The following steps to score teaching allow you to do this.

4. The following steps can be used to teach a score.

Step 1. Teach the text.

a. Note any words of the text that might be mispronounced (the singers should make pencil marks of these).

b. Recite the text on a pitch appropriate to the tessitura of the composition. Inflect according to word accents.

Step 2. Teach the rhythm.

a. Have your students mark all breaths in their scores. Where they are "cheating" notes to squeeze in a breath, mark in rests to indicate precisely how much time will be given to the breath. Leave nothing to chance.

b. Speak the rhythm on *ta ta ta* and/or *one and two and*. The difficulty of the rhythm and experience of the group determine the amount of time spent on this step.

c. Have the chorus draw in the arrows ($\downarrow$ $\uparrow$) showing where the notes coincide with the beats when rhythmic problems arise. You will have to do this on the board for them several times before they can do it. Remember, start with easy music.

d. Recite the text in rhythm with the inflections of the words and with rhythmic nuances. Recite within a pitch level comparable to the tessitura of the songs. (See Figure 11-3.)

Figure 11-3

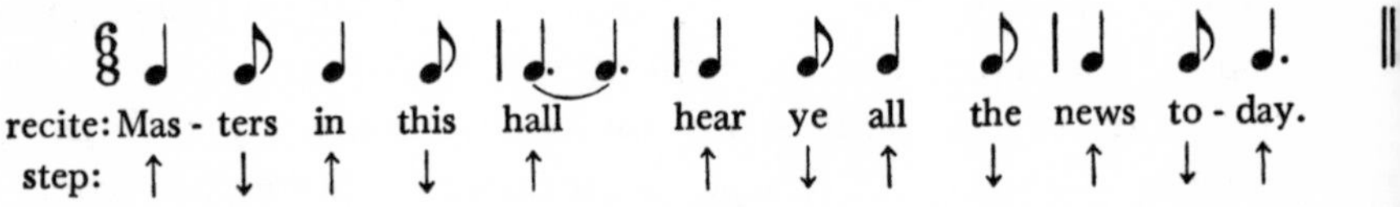

recite: Mas - ters in this hall   hear ye all   the news to - day.
step: ↑   ↓   ↑   ↓   ↑   ↑   ↓ ↑   ↓   ↑   ↓ ↑

Up arrows indicate a body lift; down arrows indicate a step by the opposite foot.

e. Step the rhythm (eurhythmics).

f. Step the rhythm while the chorus recites the text. It is not necessary to go through each of these steps for every composition. Vary the number and the order of the steps you go through. After more experience you will know which steps are needed most by your group to solve rhythmic problems.

Step 3. Teach the pitches.

a. On easy music, after the pitches are given sing the composition without any accompaniment. It is sometimes easier to sing the counting (*one and two and three and*) before coordinating the words with the pitches.

b. A variation of this is to count the rhythms as the piano plays the pitches.

c. A third approach is to have everyone learn all the parts. First have everyone sing the bass part until it sounds secure. Second, the basses stay on their part while the tenors, sopranos and altos sing the tenor part. The basses and tenors stay on their parts while all the girls sing first the alto and then the soprano. Finally, everyone sings his own part. This is an especially good approach to teaching polyphonic music.

d. Another approach to teaching pitches is to have everyone first learn the soprano (melody) line. This is helpful in teaching phrasing and nuance, especially in homophonic music.

Step 4. Check the harmony.

The harmony is checked by having the chorus change chords only on the direction of the conductor (arhythmic). Each chord is sung, after which the accompanist slowly rolls the chord from the bass upward. The singers make any corrections.

Step 5. Use silent singing to check for pitch accuracy.

Always check the accuracy of pitch learning by singing

each phrase silently and the cadence aloud. If the cadence is sung in tune by all the singers you know the pitches are secure. If the cadence is out of tune, ask your singers to tell you the pitches they could not clearly imagine.

Step 6. Teach style, dynamics and phrasing.

Step 6 should be an integral part of all the previous steps. The mood of the text, the natural text nuances, the dynamics, the style and phrase leading—all should be taught while the text, rhythm, and pitches are drilled. Work from the general to specific in presentation of interpretive ideas. Get the overall effect first and gradually (as the choristers become more secure in their notes) add refinement to the interpretation.

5. Demonstrate what you want. You don't have to have a great voice to show the students the difference between imagining sounds without hesitation compared to swelling on each note, or how a phrase should be sung (anacrusis, crusis, feminine rhythm). However, don't teach vocal quality by direct imitation. Students should imitate their own speech timbres and not that of their teacher.

6. Listen. Listen. Listen. Tune your ear in to how the chorus really sounds, not how you would like them to sound.

Conducting Hints

1. Practice conducting in front of a mirror. Practice beat patterns with both the downward (bounce) ictus and the upward (toss) ictus. Be sure each beat contains a clearly defined preparation, ictus, and reflex. Each reflex should be one-half the size of the preparation. Practice until the beat is balanced; in four-four meter, beats two and three should be equal distance from beat one. Work for refinement, poise, and overall ease and efficiency of motion. No matter how many years we conduct, it is helpful and often revealing to conduct a composition in front of a mirror before we conduct it in front of our chorus.

2. Stand on a podium in rehearsals and performances. The podium serves as a focal point for your singers. It is good to vary your distance from the chorus from time to time, but stand still once the placement of the podium is established. Moving about while you conduct is distracting and meaningless to your interpretive gestures. It also indicates a lack of confidence on your part.

The elevation of the podium depends upon the height of the conductor, but even tall conductors should use one.

3. Make conducting gestures that are intelligible. Use traditional beat patterns, not superficial, flowery ones.

4. Set the mood of each composition through your posture and facial expression before the preparatory beat begins the piece.

5. Make clear preparatory beats. The preparation sets the tempo, the dynamic level and the style of the composition. The preparation is much more important than the ictus and reflex in these respects.

6. Delineate between *marcato, staccato* and *legato* gestures. Practice in front of a mirror and use the expressive gestures consistently in rehearsals and performances. The more consistent your gestures, the more consistently your singers will respond to them.

7. Cue entrances in polyphonic texture through eye contact, a mouthed word and/or a nod of the head. Pointing with the left hand should be reserved for bringing in sections which have had a long period of rests.

8. Predetermine the length of each fermata and decide whether each is a breath fermata, a stopped fermata, or a silent pause fermata. Plan your gestures accordingly.

9. Make eye contact with your singers, keep your gestures clear and meaningful, and demand they make eye contact with you. However, never fake the knowledge of your score beyond what is actual. Look at your singers for a purpose—cueing, preparing dynamic changes, crescendos and diminuendos, a change in style, a wavering tempo, etc.

10. Conduct your accompanist on all introductions and inter-ludes. Set all tempos. Never let your accompanist lead you.

11. Keep spoken directions to a minimum. When possible, demonstrate instead of talk. Remember that choristers come to rehearsals to sing. Plan verbal explanations so they can be made with as few words as possible.

12. Set posture standards for sitting and standing. Demand these standards consistently. Watch for raised shoulders and noisy breaths. Your singers should hold their music high enough so they can see you and the music without moving their heads up and down. Every student should hold his own music—never have two persons on one copy of music.

13. Constantly listen to your chorus for accurate rhythm and pitches, purity of vowel sounds, clear consonants, and balance of parts.

14. Show how you feel about the music you are conducting. We ask our singers to release themselves mentally and emotion-ally into the involvement of singing. If we can't intuitively respond to music and show how it affects us, we can't expect our singers to respond and communicate.

Recruiting Your Chorus

No choral conductor can develop a great chorus without talented members in his group. Recruitment is one of our most important jobs. I believe in personal recruitment—speaking to individuals and showing a concern for them.

Ways To Recruit

1. In the first rehearsal of the year, discuss with the chorus your plans for the year: the concerts you are planning, the Christmas carol-sing, the spring festival, the exchange program with a nearby school—and your dreams. Encourage each member to speak to his friends about chorus and its potential

under your leadership. Get a list of names of the individuals the chorus feels would be an asset to the chorus and *contact each one personally*.

2. Go into each study hall and let the young people know about the choral program you envision.

3. Many students will point out schedule conflicts that "can't be worked out." Guidance directors want young people (especially boys) in the choral program. Convince your guidance director you mean business. Go into his office with each prospect and work out each scheduling difficulty. The changes a guidance director will make in scheduling to accommodate students are sometimes pleasantly surprising.

4. This is humbling—but I've done it. Stand in the hall between classes and personally invite every mature boy that comes along to join chorus. I've had some pretty negative reactions from this style of recruiting, such as—What are you, some kind of a nut?" But there were some who have said—"Thank you, I would really like that." These boys make it worthwhile.

5. Football teams always contain many good singers. You can't beat them, so join them. Making friends with the coaching staff can be a tremendous help. A male director can go down on the field and throw the ball around with the boys. A woman director can't throw the ball around but she can go to the games and show an active interest in the sports program. Would we want anything less for our music program?

Recruiting is a full time job, and not an easy one. Sometimes it's humbling, but that's the way it's done—through your belief in your program, talking your ideas up, making personal contacts, and by having a real concern for young people.

Index

215